If Not You, Who?

It's Your Life
Make It Count

Don O'Neal

Published by DONeal imprints
Springfield, IL

Based on the belief that we can do almost anything we set our minds to, if we believe in ourselves, and dare to dream.

Also available,
If Not Now, When?

Printed in the United States of America

Cover design by David Waugh

Editing: Rhonda K. O'Neal

ISBN-13:978-0692212905

DEDICATION

To my Mom and Dad, brothers and sisters, my wife, Nancy, our children and grandchildren, and all of our extended families. So much of whatever I am and who I am I owe to you and our love for each other, for which I'm forever in your debt.

A special thanks to my daughter, Rhonda, for your editing expertise, patience, and time

Don O'Neal

Table of Contents

Don O'Neal

INTRODUCTION

"This above all: to thine own self be true,
and it must follow, as the night the day,
thou canst not then be false to any man."
(Shakespeare, from Hamlet)

"Life has no meaning
except in terms of responsibility."
(Reinhold Niebuhr, 1892-1971)

How do you feel about your life: about where you are compared with where you'd like to be? Are you satisfied with the way things are, or do you feel there's something missing? What are your hopes and plans for the future? Are you comfortable with where you're going, and confident you'll get there? Or do you even think about the future?

The way we feel about ourselves affects everything about us: our attitude, enthusiasm, and perhaps most important, our self-esteem. So it's a good idea once in a while to stop and think about what you're doing, what you're accomplishing, where you're heading, and what the future holds for you.

You can choose what you want to do with your life. Your purpose, integrity, sense of responsibility, and the opportunities you find will be what give meaning to whatever you do. And whatever you do is all up to you.

As you read on, you'll notice the repeated use of statements like, *"It's your life"* or *"It's all up to you."*

That's because what happens in your life and to your life is entirely your responsibility. It's you who will be responsible for your success or frustration. It's you who will be responsible for whether you move forward or stay where you are. And it's you who will be responsible for whether or not you will ultimately be happy. In the end, if you don't take responsibility for yourself, who will?

While there are those who don't believe there's anything they can do about the future, the truth is there's a *lot* you can do about it. You can plan the future you want and make it happen, but it's all up to *you*. If *you* don't do it, who will?

You can do whatever you set your mind to, become whatever you decide to, get whatever your heart desires. But you have to *know* exactly what you want and believe you can get it.

Philosophers have insisted that what we want most from life is happiness, but they've never agreed on what *makes* us happy or even what happiness *is.*

Some say happiness is having everything we want; realizing all of our desires. (Epicurus)

Others suggest the opposite: that happiness is being content with what we *have*, no matter how little it may be. (Seneca)

Still others argue that happiness can only come from living a meaningful life; achieving our highest purpose in life. (Aristotle)

So if you want to be happy, what should you do? Work hard to get everything you want? Try to be satisfied with what you have? Live a meaningful life?

The first approach is likely to be an exercise in futility. Getting something we want can make us feel good for a while, but only temporarily, because usually soon after we get it, we'll be thinking about what's next: what *more* we want. So we'll never be satisfied for long.

That means we really only have two choices for happiness: being content with whatever we have or finding a way to live a meaningful life.

Being content with what we have is a sensible and perhaps ideal form of happiness, but contentment won't work for everyone because many of us are inherently strivers, always trying to improve our situations.

You, for example, probably wouldn't be reading this book if you weren't looking for ways to improve yourself and/or your life, and I certainly wouldn't have written it if I wasn't that kind of person. So for you and me and others like us, living a meaningful life is likely to be the best way to find happiness.

Of course, it's important to recognize that happiness is likely to be more a journey than a destination:

"Happiness is a process, a continual becoming, in which we rise to our full potential by fully realizing ourselves." (St. Thomas Aquinas)

"Those only are happy who have their minds fixed on some object other than their own happiness; on the happiness of others, on the improvement of mankind, even on some art or pursuit, followed not as a means, but as itself an ideal end. Aiming, thus, at something else, they find happiness by the way." (John Stuart Mill)

So following this path means believing you have a purpose in life and that your best chance at happiness is to find your purpose and pursue it. How do you do that? Perhaps a parable can give you some food for thought:

In biblical times, when cities were protected by walls, a traveling rabbi finally reached his destination late in the evening, only to find the city closed for the night. When he pounded on the gates and asked to be let in, a voice from the darkness demanded:

"Who are you?"
"Why are you here?"

As the rabbi was thinking about how to answer, again came the voice:
"Who are you?"
"Why are you here?"

This time the rabbi did respond, but with a question of his own:
"How much do they pay you?"

After the voice had told him, the rabbi called back:
"I'll pay you twice that much to come work for me."

To which the voice called back:
"What would you have me do?"

The rabbi replied:
"Just ask me those two questions every morning when I wake up:
"Who are you?"
"Why are you here?"

So a good way for you to begin would be to ask yourself two similar questions:
"Who am I?"
"Why am I here?"

Then let this book guide you through the process of thinking about your life and what you can do to make it more meaningful, more satisfying.

It will help you take an objective look at yourself, determine what you can do that will give you the greatest pride and sense of accomplishment in the years to come, and most important, begin the actions and activities that will make it all happen.

I've been successful in three different careers -- engineer, corporate executive, and professor -- and a lot of what I accomplished was because I always took *personal responsibility* for myself.

I had been fortunate to learn, early on, that *I* am responsible for everything I do, and I alone -- not someone else -- am accountable for my actions. That means that whatever happens to me and whether I succeed or fail in whatever I do is mainly up to me.

And I've helped a number of young people develop their own careers and had the pleasure of seeing how by taking personal responsibility for themselves they've enriched not only their careers, but their personal lives as well.

So if you want to make the most of *your* life, you can start, right now, by facing up to three responsibilities that you have: 1) *to* yourself; 2) *for* yourself; and 3) to *others*.

1) Responsibility *to* yourself means being true to yourself; following *your* dreams; becoming what and who *you* want to be, not what someone else thinks you should be. You owe it to yourself to be the best that you can be, and you can only do that by following *your* passion and doing what's most important to *you*.

PART I – PURPOSE (Responsibility *to* yourself)

Chapter 1. CHOICE

Chapter 2. VISION
                    Meaning
                    Direction

Chapter 3. PERSISTENCE
                    Desire
                    Believing

2) Responsibility *for* yourself means taking responsibility for the consequences of your actions. To do that, you'll need to be humble, objective, and honest with yourself so you can recognize and admit your errors, mistakes and failures, and use them for self-improvement.

3) Responsibility to *others* means living your life in such a way that you become an example: the kind of person others will want to look up to and respect.

And perhaps most important, you have to *believe* in yourself and believe that you have a responsibility to live your life to the fullest. This book will show you how to do that: how to begin living your life in a way that will make you feel good about yourself and what you're doing and give you the comfort of knowing that someday, when you look back on your life, you will be proud of who you were and how you lived.

It's all up to you. You can do anything you set your mind to: become whatever you want to, get whatever your heart desires. How successful you are will depend on:

1) your *purpose*;
2) your personal *integrity*;
3) your sense of *responsibility*; and
4) your *opportunities*.

Don O'Neal

Part I – Purpose
Responsibility *to* yourself

Your purpose is the reason you exist: what you intend to do with your life. Your purpose should be something you believe in so passionately that it focuses what you do, where you go, and even who you are. Purpose is what gives your life meaning, direction, and commitment.

Chapter 1 is about *choice*: choosing what you want to do with your life, then making things happen *for* you rather than settling for whatever happens *to* you. Chapter 2 discusses the importance of *vision*: how to develop a clear picture of the future you want -- a vision that will give direction and meaning to everything you do. Chapter 3 is about *persistence*: the commitment you'll need to keep following your vision in spite of any obstacles you may have to overcome.

But just having a purpose isn't enough; you have to *do* something about it, take action, do what's necessary to make it a reality. And only *you* can make that happen. It isn't something you can leave to others.

Part II – Integrity
Responsibility *for* yourself

Your personal integrity defines what kind of person you are: what you believe in, what you do, and how you do it. Personal integrity can increase your self-confidence and effectiveness and make

14

you either an inspiration for others or the kind of person others find it difficult to depend on.

Chapter 4 is about *character:* the foundation of integrity. Your character is based on the kind of person you are and the values and ethics that guide your behavior. Chapter 5 discusses *credibility*: how believable others feel you are. Your credibility comes from your self-awareness, consistency, and trustworthiness.

Chapter 6 emphasizes the importance of *attitude*: your outlook on life, how you think, how you feel about yourself and about others, how you present yourself.

With integrity, your opportunities are unlimited; without it, your prospects will be dim. It's all up to you. The choice of what kind of person you become is your responsibility, and yours alone.

Part III – Responsibility
Responsibility to *others*

Note, I said responsibility *to* others, not *for* them. That means you are responsible for *your* actions -- for how you treat others -- but *not* for *their* actions or what *they* do.

Chapter 7 is about *duty*: your moral obligations. Doing your duty requires recognizing your obligations, then unselfishly doing what is *right* rather than what is easiest.

Chapter 8 discusses *respect*: the importance of our regard for others and the consideration we show in our actions toward them.

Chapter 9 discusses how difficult *communication* can be unless we make an effort to understand the other person's point of view. Chapter 10 is about the importance of the *example* we set by what we do and how we do it. What others *see* us do is more often the basis of their opinion of us than anything we *say*.

Part IV – Opportunity

The ability to recognize *opportunities* can have a huge influence on your future. Almost any situation we encounter can be viewed as either a threat or an opportunity, depending on how we look at it. With confidence in yourself and a positive attitude, you will begin to see opportunities where others see only threats.

Chapter 11 discusses *foresight*: the ability to see trends, and analyze the opportunities they present. Chapter 12 is about *focus*: choosing which opportunities to pursue and which to let go. Focus requires setting goals and making tradeoffs.

Chapter 13 discusses your *capabilities*: your knowledge, skills, and abilities and how they can be either strengths or weaknesses. Success in your chosen career will have a lot to do with how well you identify and develop your unique capabilities.

Chapter 14 emphasizes the importance of *action*. Planning how to achieve your goals is important, but taking the actions necessary to achieve them is absolutely essential. It's safe to say that a majority of people who have dreams and plans never do anything beyond dreaming. They never take the actions necessary to make those dreams come true, usually because they simply can't bring themselves to make the necessary decisions or to take action. We'll help make sure you're not one of those people.

Chapter 15 is about *courage*: the ability to face your fears and overcome them. And here we're talking about *moral* courage, not physical courage: the courage to do the right thing rather than what's popular. This kind of courage requires making the *right* choices, committing to the *best* courses of action, and being willing to make whatever sacrifices those actions require.

A final note of introduction: as you read through the chapters that follow, it's important to understand one thing about me, your writer. I am, first and foremost, a teacher, and that helps define me in whatever I do or write.

In the classroom, my primary goal is to engage students, to arouse their interest in the subject at hand. That isn't always easy, as many college students return to the classroom after a gap of several years between high school and college. That means to get their attention and keep their interest, I have to do much more than just lecture; I have to find ways to get them involved in class discussions.

Over time, I've found that what works best for me is to illustrate our discussions with "real world" examples, from my own experience as well as from theirs. As you've probably noticed in your own life, our most intense personal experiences leave lasting imprints on us and often become the foundations of our strongest opinions.

As new students in my class quickly learn, I have a number of those opinions, which I refer to as my "soapbox issues because as I discuss them, I'm likely to express them more emphatically and lecture longer than I had intended. Of course, I realize that not everyone will agree with my perspective, so I always emphasize to students that these are *my* opinions, not necessarily theirs, and they always seem to understand.

For that reason, I hope my readers will understand when you are (occasionally) treated to one of my "soapbox issues" in the chapters that follow. You'll notice that some of them are repeated, sometimes more than once, so I'll tell you what I remind my students: when you see me repeating myself, it does not (necessarily) mean I'm becoming senile. I'm simply reinforcing those issues that I consider fundamentals: things I feel are essential to remember.

As you move on through the book, I urge you: don't just read what I've written, but try to envision, chapter by chapter, topic by topic, how the principles that have enriched my life can help bring meaning to yours.

PART I - PURPOSE

In this section we discuss purpose, by which we mean *your* purpose -- *what you intend to do with your life.*

Your future can be a *dream,* or it can be a *vision.* The difference? A dream is something you think about and wish for, while a vision is a clear picture of what you want and a plan for getting it.

The difference between a dream and a vision is *action* -- *doing* something about it. Why do some people just dream while others do whatever it takes to make their vision a reality?

It has a lot to do with *desire* – how badly we want something. The power of a purpose comes from our desire to get things that we value. What might those things be? It varies from one person to another.

Aristotle, for example, classified the things we value most into two categories: *internal* goods, which includes health, beauty, strength, physical stature, athletic ability, and virtue; and *external* goods, which includes friends, money, honor, fame, and luck.

More recently, psychologist Abraham Maslow suggested that we value things in terms of our *needs*, which he classified into five levels in order of their importance to us: physiological, safety, love, esteem, and self-actualization.

Although any one of the values on Aristotle's list could become a person's driving purpose in life, none are likely to be stronger than Maslow's highest level of needs: self-actualization. And it's from Maslow's perspective that we'll discuss purpose: having a purpose that gives meaning to your life.

Now, your purpose in life may not be obvious to you, and it isn't likely to miraculously appear to you. You will have to develop your own purpose through *your* decisions and actions.

First, you have to make a *choice*: you must choose to take control of your life, to make things happen *for* you instead of just sitting back and letting things happen *to* you.

Next, you'll need a *vision*: a clear picture of the future you desire, a future that will give direction and meaning to everything you do.

Finally, you'll have to have *persistence*: a commitment to stay the course regardless of any obstacles you may have to overcome.

Don O'Neal

1. CHOICE

*"To be what we are, and to become
what we are capable of becoming,
is the only end of life."*

(Robert Louis Stevenson, 1850-1894)

We all make many choices in our lives, but many people fail to see the need for the one choice that matters most: how to live their lives. We can either let the future – our own future – happen by chance, or we can make it happen the way we want it to. Either way, it's a choice: we can do nothing or we can do something.

Each of us has the opportunity to determine our personal future: to make things happen the way we want; to achieve the things that we desire, the things that matter most to us; to live the life we choose. We can do that by choosing what we want, then doing whatever is necessary to get it.

Unfortunately, many people don't choose that path; in fact, they don't choose any path at all. They just drift along, letting life and circumstances make their choices for them.

I've often wondered why that is: why some people seem willing to take whatever fate hands them. Is it luck, fate, or an accident of birth: where, when, or to whom we were born?

I'm not sure it's any of those, although circumstances make life more difficult for some people than for others. And I don't believe it's because some people work harder than others. We've all seen people who work hard all their lives and wind up with little, while others hardly seem to work at all but have great success. So if it's none of those, what is it that makes some people *choose* how to live their lives while others don't? I think it really comes down to how we *think*, and what we *believe*.

Some people drift through life because they don't think they have a choice in the matter. They don't really believe they can influence what happens to them. Of course, it's *possible* for them to change the way they think, but it probably won't happen until they come to *believe* they really do have a choice.

Others' lives are influenced by people they respect, either from their advice or by how they are living *their* lives.

In either case, once we start down that path, inertia takes over, and the longer we follow that path, the more difficult it is to change. It's hard to overcome inertia -- to move in a different direction -- because it means getting out of our comfortable rut and sometimes even doing the opposite of those around us, thereby spotlighting ourselves as being *different*.

Changing doesn't have to be as difficult as it may seem, although it often means stepping outside of your comfort zone, which may involve some uncertainty. It's much more difficult to change if you're trying to do it because someone else wants you to. But if you genuinely *want* to change, you can. Here's how it's done.

First you have to realize that where you are right now is a result of the choices you've made or because you *haven't made* choices. Either way, it's been up to you. If you've made good choices and you're heading in the direction you want to go, you probably feel good about yourself. And if whatever you're doing seems to be working and moving you toward your destination, you should keep it up.

But if you don't feel like you're heading in the right direction because of some choices you've made -- some choices that didn't work out -- it's time to put the past behind you and begin believing that your future can be different. It can be whatever you make it.

You can begin by asking yourself, "Where do I want to go from here? What kind of person do I want to become? Who do I want to be?"

Your answers will depend on how you see yourself. If you see yourself as average, ordinary, run-of-the-mill, you'll have to change that way of thinking right now because you're *not* ordinary; nobody is. You just haven't recognized your possibilities.

You need to start telling yourself that you're *not* ordinary and that you don't have to settle for what you've always had or for the same things other people are content with. You can be whatever you want to be, whoever you want to be, and you can do whatever you want to do. But discarding your old self-image may not be easy, especially if you've believed it for a long time.

In fact, it may be quite difficult at first, but it will become easier as you begin to see and feel the results. This step can be challenging because it takes you in a different direction, and a new direction always involves a good deal of uncertainty, some initial discomfort, and perhaps some risk.

But in reality, it usually isn't all that risky; it just looks that way because you've never been there before. It's uncharted territory. And one of the reasons so many people are afraid to do it is because it's easier and more comfortable to keep on doing what you've always done than it is to make the effort and take the risk of trying something new.

While it may be easier and more comfortable to remain just one of the faceless multitude -- to blend in with the crowd -- that's never the road to personal success. Pride, satisfaction, and success come from striving to be better than just "good enough" by setting high standards for yourself.

The key to believing in yourself is to have a vision: a vibrant picture of a bright new future and a new *you*. In the next chapter, we'll talk more about your vision, but the important thing to know right now is that to *get* somewhere with your life, you have to be *going* somewhere: some special destination that's so important and compelling that you'll do whatever it takes to get there.

Summary

How you live your life is up to you; it's your choice. Everything we've discussed in this chapter, and that will be discussed in the chapters that follow, depends on your willingness to *choose* the life you want rather than settling for whatever life hands you. Of course, there's nothing that says you *have* to choose the life you want to live; you can always take the easy way and choose *not* to choose.

And if you decide you'd rather just sit back and take what life hands you -- do what the rest of the crowd is doing, go with the flow -- you can disregard the rest of this section all together. What's here is only meaningful if you want to *choose* your future and *know* where you're going and how to get there.

If you don't care where you go, nothing you do will matter all that much; any direction will do, and any destination will be as good as any other. The only problem is that you may never know where you *are*, where you're *going*, or *what* you'll get when you arrive. But then you probably won't care, will you?

Life is pretty much what we make it. Every day, when you wake up, you have a choice of what kind of day you're going to have. Why not choose to make it a good day? If you do that, and do it every day, you're almost sure to have a good life no matter what you choose to do or who you choose to be.

2. VISION

"Vision looks inward and becomes duty.
Vision looks outward and becomes aspiration.
Vision looks upward and becomes faith."
(Stephen S. Wise, 1874-1949)

As we discussed in Chapter 1, your future is up to you: you can plan your own destiny, or you can just sit back and wait for whatever happens to you. I hope the fact that you've moved on to this chapter means you *have* made a choice and decided to create the future you desire; one that will take you where you want to go.

If so, the next thing you'll need is a *vision*: a clear picture of where you want to go, what you want to become. The dictionary defines vision as, "A mental image produced by the imagination…"

I prefer to look at vision as "… similar to a dream, except a dream is more like a wish – something we hope for - while a vision is a clear picture of a desired outcome, along with a plan for what has to be done to turn it into a reality." "A vision clarifies where we want to go, what we intend to accomplish, and why. It gives us a sense of purpose, and focuses our attention and efforts. Following a vision gives meaning and direction to our lives, our jobs, and our daily activities." (O'Neal, 2009: 29)

So your vision should be a clear mental picture of the future you desire along with an idea of how you intend to make that future possible. Your vision may become your main purpose in life and will bring *meaning* to your work and your life. It should be so clear in your mind that you will always know in which *direction* you're heading and what you'll find when you get there.

Meaning

Professor Mihaly Czikszentmihalyi suggests, "People who find their lives meaningful usually have a goal that is challenging enough to take up all of their energies, a goal that can give significance to their lives. We may refer to this process as achieving *purpose.* " He goes on to say that answering the question, "What is the meaning of life?" is quite simple, "The meaning of life *is* meaning: whatever it is, wherever it comes from, a unified purpose of life is what gives meaning to life." (1990:216, 217)

To help you envision what might give meaning to your work and your life, we'll use Dr. Abraham Maslow's hierarchy of needs, because it demonstrates so well why, in our jobs and careers, most of us would much prefer to do meaningful work rather than those boring, repetitive, and sometimes useless tasks that often take up the majority of our work life.

Maslow believed five sets of needs motivate human behavior and help explain much of what we do and why we do it. He viewed those needs as "hierarchical" in the sense that our *basic* needs are most critical and will dominate our attention and efforts until they have been satisfied. Then, and only then, will our attention shift to the level above.

Those needs are shown below as a set of steps, beginning with our physiological needs.

Self-Actualization
(fulfillment)

Esteem (respect, appreciation, importance)

Social (belonging, friendship, affection, love)

Safety (protection from the elements enemies, illness, accidents, disease)

Physiological (water, food, procreation)

Water, food, and the ability to reproduce are our most basic needs, and until those needs have been satisfied, we will think about little else.

But once those needs have been met – our thirst has been quenched, our hunger sated, and we feel free to have children – our attention will move up to the second step: *safety*.

We will focus on our safety needs until we have shelter from the weather, protection from our enemies, and are able to avoid accidents, illness, and disease. Only then will our attention shift to the next step: our *social* needs.

Social needs – the desire to belong to something or someone - are among the most powerful drivers of behavior. We all crave friendship, affection, and love and will do almost anything in our power to get them.

It's important to note that at this level, we've moved above issues of survival to needs that are still important but less tangible. Needs at this level could be considered "wants" or "desires" rather than needs, as we don't need them to survive, but they may be essential for us to *thrive*.

Once our social needs have been satisfied, we step up to *esteem*: our desire to be respected, appreciated, and feel important. We all crave the attention we feel we deserve for our accomplishments; although this need may not be essential to our survival, it can be vitally important to our attitude, enthusiasm, and self-confidence.

Maslow's perspective on the importance of esteem is strongly reinforced by surveys of workers in which they repeatedly and consistently insist that doing work that is *important* is what gives them satisfaction in their jobs and gives meaning to their work and careers.

Maslow saw *self-actualization* as the final step of his hierarchy because when all is said and done, we need meaning in more than just our jobs; we need to know that our *lives* have meaning -- that we're making a difference.

Although some people lament that life has no meaning, Prof. Czikszentmihalyi does not agree. "Much of what we call culture and civilization consists in efforts people have made, generally against overwhelming odds, to create a sense of purpose for themselves and their descendents."

He goes on to suggest that, "From the point of view of the individual, it does not matter what the ultimate goal is – providing it is compelling enough to order a lifetime's worth of psychic energy.... As long as it provides clear objectives, clear rules for action, and a way to concentrate and become involved, any goal can serve to give meaning to a person's life."(1990: 215)

So both meaning and satisfaction come from knowing that what we're doing is important, not just routine. And, as a side note to those interested in leadership, research clearly demonstrates that a key element in effective leadership is the ability to help others find *meaning* in what they do.

Considering what we've discussed so far and what you now know about our different levels of needs, you may have realized that this book is primarily directed at those who have progressed beyond the two most basic levels of needs, those who are no longer primarily concerned with hunger, homelessness, or fear for their lives.

Might they still want more – a nicer home, a better car, more money? Of course. They may *always* want more. But their needs have evolved to where they're no longer fighting for survival.

So this book is focused on helping address the top three levels of needs: social, esteem, and self-actualization, none of which can be satisfied by things – by how much you own. It is not as concerned with helping you get more of what you have as it is with helping you find meaning in your work and your life.

At this point, the questions you should be asking are "How do I get from where I am to where I want to be?" "How do I start pursuing my vision so I can find meaning in what I do?" -- which leads us to the subject of *direction*.

Direction

Although the word has several meanings, the definition that fits our purpose is "the line or course along which a person or thing moves."

Any time you decide to go somewhere – it doesn't matter where – you first have to decide *where* you want to go: "What's my destination?" Once you have a vision, you've answered the "Where?" question, so you know your destination.

Next you have to decide *how*: How do you get from where you are to where you want to be? There are two parts to that question. First, "What actions, activities, methods, etc. are necessary to achieve my vision?" Answering that question will be the subject of a later chapter.

The second part of the question and the one on which we're focusing in this chapter is about *direction*: "What route or path will get me from here to there -- from where I am to where I want to be?" No matter how clearly you can picture your destination, if you don't know which direction to go to get there, you're almost certain to waste time and effort taking unnecessary detours.

But before you can decide which direction to go, you have to know where you *are:* what's your starting point? Until you know where you *are*, you have no way of knowing what direction to go to get *anywhere*. Consider the following example:

A hot-air balloonist is drifting peacefully over the countryside on a beautiful summer afternoon when he's suddenly drawn into a violent thunderstorm. Buffeted around for what seems like hours, uncertain of where he is and fearful that he might be destined for a painful if not fatal landing, he is quite relieved when sometime later he regains consciousness, still in his gondola, which is lying on its side in a field.

He sits up, rubbing his head, and is looking around to see where he has landed when he sees a man running toward him shouting, "Are you all right? Are you all right?"

The balloonist ponders that for a minute, then replies, "Yes, I seem to be quite all right, but where am I?"

To which his would-be rescuer responds, "You're in a basket in the middle of a field."

The balloonist considers that for a moment, then answers, "I don't want to seem ungrateful, but the information you've given me, though absolutely correct, is completely useless."

The reason for the balloonist's frustration will be obvious to anyone who has ever been lost, whether in a city, on a highway, or a country road. The fact that we know we're in a car and on a road is completely useless unless we know where the road *is*. Only then can we determine which way to go to get to our destination.

That's why every shopping-mall directory has a "You are here" indicator, as does the map on the wall in every highway rest area.

So determining your direction requires not only knowing your destination (where you want to *go*) but also your current location (where you *are* right now).

Is direction always important? Only if you have a particular destination in mind. If you aren't going anywhere in particular or don't care where you go, direction may not matter at all. But for anyone with a vision, direction is a critical step in fulfilling that vision. Our vision gives us the meaning that drives us forward. Direction shows us the path to that destination.

Summary

Vision is the way we picture the kind of future that will give meaning to our lives. Meaning is what drives us – it's *why* we do what we do. Direction is what keeps us heading toward that future and helps us avoid meaningless distractions along the way.

That's why having a clear picture of the future is so important. The knowledge that our efforts will achieve meaningful results provides the kind of inspiration that stimulates our enthusiasm. With a vision, we know exactly where we're going, why we're going there, and we have a compelling picture of what we'll get when we arrive.

But without a clear idea of where we're going, or *why* we're going there, when there's no clear outcome to aim for, no good reason for what we're doing, no purpose, no meaning, what will we have to look forward to?

Don O'Neal

3. PERSISTENCE

*"Success is to be measured not so much
by the position that one has reached in life
as by the obstacles which one has overcome…"*
(Booker T. Washington, 1856-1915)

What is persistence, and what does it have to do with *purpose*? The American Heritage Dictionary defines "persist" as "to hold steadfastly to a purpose or undertaking despite obstacles." In other words, persistence is sticking with a task until it's completed.

Without persistence, we are likely to become discouraged by difficulties and may turn back when we encounter any kind of resistance. Life is full of obstacles, and if we don't have the persistence to overcome them, we aren't likely to get anywhere. So there's a direct connection between persistence and accomplishment: the greater our persistence, the more obstacles we'll overcome, and the more we'll accomplish.

President Calvin Coolidge said this:

"Nothing in the world can take the place of persistence. Talent will not; nothing is more

common than unsuccessful men with great talent. Genius will not; unrewarded genius is almost a proverb. Education will not; the world is full of educated derelicts. Persistence, determination alone are omnipotent."

Now let's look at persistence in the context of purpose. We've said that the first step toward purpose is *choice*: consciously choosing what you want your future to be, rather than just accepting whatever happens to you, whatever comes along.

Next you need a *vision* – a clear picture of what that future will look like. But neither choosing your future nor having a vision of what it will look like are enough.

Your vision will never be more than a dream if you don't have the *persistence* to make it a reality no matter what it takes and in spite of whatever you have to go through to get there.

Persistence ensures that you *will* make your vision a reality; that you *will* stick with it until you get there; that you won't let anything get in your way. Where does such persistence come from, and why do some people have it while others don't?

I believe every one of us is endowed with persistence, although the depth of it varies considerably from one person to another. Persistence is largely mental, and the strength of it can range from complete disinterest to total obsession.

The two most important things that influence persistence are *desire* and *belief*. Desire is how badly we *want* or crave something, and belief is how much faith we have that we *can* achieve what we desire, and make our vision a reality.

This isn't something new; I'm sure you've done it before. Stop for a minute and think back to a time when you felt this way -- when you wanted something so much you would do almost anything to get it.

When did you feel that way? *What* made you feel that way?

Desire

Desire is driven by *need*. The more we need something, the stronger our desire. But it can also be driven by *want*, although we often want things that we don't really need.

Strangely, the dictionary definitions don't do much to differentiate between need and want; it uses them interchangeably, utilizing one to define the other. But in keeping with our discussion of Maslow's perspective on needs in the previous chapter, we'll use these definitions:

Need – something *necessary,* required for our physical or mental *well-being.* (i.e., survival, safety, security, protection)

Want – something we'd *like to have* for personal *satisfaction* or *comfort.* (i.e., love, friendship, belonging, recognition, appreciation)

To me, the *strength* of our desire is probably more important than whether it's driven by a need or a want. The more we desire something, the more likely we are to have the persistence to achieve it regardless of whether it's something we really do need or just something we want badly.

Believing

We tend to believe something because we have confidence in it, and our level of confidence is often based on past experience. The adage, "Seeing is believing" is based on the fact that we're more likely to believe something we've actually seen or have personally experienced than something we've only heard about from someone else.

For example, when we flip a light-switch, we expect a light to come on. We are confident the light will come on; in fact, we *know* it will come on, because it always *has*. Knowing is perhaps the strongest form of believing. We don't just believe it will happen; there's no question in our mind that it *will* happen. We're absolutely certain.

Impossible -- ? -- Possible -- Probable -- Certain
(Disbelief)   (Belief)
Belief

The diagram above shows the relative strength of a person's belief, from believing something is impossible at one extreme to believing it's a certainty at the other. Using the light-switch analogy, we are *certain* the light will come on because it always has.

It stands to reason that if our confidence is based on how strongly we believe in something, our *self*-confidence is based on how strongly we believe in *ourselves*. And it makes sense that our self-confidence in our ability to do a particular thing will be based on whether or not we've done it before and how successfully.

Our self-confidence is influenced by our failures and successes. For a person with little self-confidence, success can help build confidence, while failure is likely to diminish it even further. Someone who is highly self-confident, on the other hand, is more likely to view any failure as a natural part of the learning experience and not a reflection on his abilities. As a result, he can move past his failures and gain more experience, which further increases his self-confidence.

And the greater your self-confidence, the more likely you are to keep raising your sights to the point where you may someday believe that your potential is unlimited -- that you can do anything you set your mind to.

Indeed, positive experience can help you progress from complete disbelief to absolute certainty, to where you have complete confidence in yourself even though you may have been a non-believer in the beginning.

Most people can overcome far more than they think they can, as in this astonishing true-life example:

Jean-Dominique Bauby, the editor of a French magazine, suffered a stroke that left him completely paralyzed at the age of 43. His condition was described as "locked-in syndrome," in which the patient is totally paralyzed, unable to move or speak.

Bauby's case was so severe that the only part of his entire body he could control was his left eyelid. Thus blinking one eye became his only means of communication.

Once he had accepted the fact that his impairment was permanent, Bauby decided to write a book. Now, just stop for a minute and think of the audacity – a person who can neither move nor speak attempting to write a book! Impossible! But he was one of those rare people for whom the impossible is just a bigger challenge.

Bauby's speech therapist developed a communication code for him so that using his only remaining tools – his hearing and the ability to blink one eye – he could dictate to a secretary. His secretary would read the alphabet to him, one letter at a time, until she came to the next letter he needed in the word he was trying to communicate. As soon as he heard that letter, he would blink.

Using his still-agile mind, Bauby created a new kind of alphabet – non-linear – to speed up the process. He rearranged the letters to use them in the order of their frequency in the French language: E S A R I N T U L O M D P C F B V H G J Q Z Y X K W. With the secretary reciting the alphabet in that order, the most-used letters would come up sooner, speeding up the spelling process, thus increasing his daily writing output considerably.

Even so, you can imagine how painfully slow writing was, with the secretary having to recite as many as 26 letters before she could type a single letter of the alphabet. One word might take several minutes and a sentence perhaps an hour or more, so a full day of writing was likely to produce no more than a paragraph or two.

Yet amazingly, Mr. Bauby completed his book. *The Diving Bell and the Butterfly*, and had it published in 1997. It is his account of the challenges he faced and how he overcame them -- an example of persistence and self-confidence that is almost impossible to imagine.

Summary

It's easy to get where you're going when everything goes according to plan. But it seldom does, and when things go wrong is when some people give up and turn back. That's why it's important to understand that the path to our vision won't always be straight, will seldom be smooth, may often be uphill, and is likely to be littered with speed-bumps, barriers, and detours.

So persistence is absolutely essential. Without it, you'll never get there. With it, you can accomplish just about anything you set your mind to.

Some may see persistence as stubbornness, and it's true that the more stubborn you are, the more persistent you are likely to be. So perhaps we need to be stubborn, but only to a point. Beyond a certain point, stubbornness can keep us doing something long after it's obvious that it isn't going to work. Unfortunately, some people won't admit to failure even when it's obvious to them.

Perhaps they're afraid of being seen as "quitters"; they don't want others to see them as failures. But it may also be that they have so much invested in time, energy, money, emotions, or reputation that they can't bear the thought of losing it, so they refuse to give up. Whatever the reason, it's important to recognize when your actions have gone beyond persistence to plain stubbornness.

But that's not easy, because it's difficult to determine what is rational and what isn't. What's rational to one person may seem positively "crazy" to another, because rationality depends on your point of view.

That's why people who don't conform to those around them, whether in thought or deed, are too often viewed as unreasonable, irrational, odd, or even crazy. And stubbornness can certainly get a person categorized under one or more of those classifications. But then, so can uniqueness, innovation, creativity, imagination, and even being unsociable.

So how can we determine when we've reached the point of irrational stubbornness? How can we know when to stop pursuing a losing proposition?

How can we know when we've crossed over from persistent to irrational?

A good way is to plan in advance the point at which you will abandon a particular action, activity, or plan -- the point at which it will be apparent that it is futile to continue. Then if or when you reach that point, you will be able to give it up no matter how hard some inner voice keeps trying to goad you on.

But you also have to be careful not to give up too easily. So it might be useful, any time things become so difficult that you're considering giving up, to remind yourself of the remarkable persistence of Jean-Dominique Bauby: "Would he have given up in my situation?"

Don O'Neal

PART II - INTEGRITY

Integrity is defined as, "honesty and independence; completeness; unity, soundness." It is strongly influenced by a person's *character* and is the basis of his/her *credibility*.

Your credibility is how *others see you* -- how trustworthy they feel you are – and is based largely on your actions. Your character is who you *are*: what you believe in, and how those beliefs affect your actions.

Integrity guides our behavior: what we do and how we do it. What we *say* means little if it isn't backed up by our behavior, because people usually form their impressions of us by how they see us behave. And if ever our actions betray our words, people are much more likely to believe what they see us do than what we say or, as Ralph Waldo Emerson put it:

"What you are stands over you the while, and thunders so that I cannot hear what you say to the contrary."

Everything we do – every action we take – either reinforces our integrity or tears it down. We should always assume that *everything* we do is almost certain to be seen by *somebody,* no matter how discrete we may think we are.

So it's best to assume that you cannot get by with *anything*. That means you should always act as though whatever you're doing is visible to everyone. And never forget: it takes a long time to build integrity but only one action, one wrong decision, to destroy it.

Above all, remember that integrity isn't situational; you either live it every day in every situation, or you lose it. You either have integrity all the time, in all circumstances, or you won't have it at all.

The chapters in this section discuss the primary foundations of integrity: *character, credibility,* and *attitude.*

Don O'Neal

4. CHARACTER

"Reputation is what men and women think of us; character is what God and angels know of us."
(Thomas Paine, 1737-1809)

Most of us tend to separate the people we know into two categories: those we can trust and those we can't. The difference is based on our perception of character.

The dictionary defines character as, "The moral or ethical structure of a person..."

Character is built on values -- the values that guide our behavior, decisions, and actions.

Our character can be developed by choice or by chance. We can consciously *choose* what kind of person we want to be, or we can just let our character develop on its own.

People with good character usually have strong, positive values that give them a good sense of right and wrong, and they base their decisions and actions on those values.

On the other hand, when a person's character develops by chance, it may be because he didn't think character was important, or he had just never thought about character. But you *should* think

Don O'Neal

about it, because your values, or lack of values, will influence every part of your life, everything you do, and perhaps most important, whether or not others will trust you.

Unfortunately, when character evolves on its own, it's likely to follow the easiest route – the path of least resistance -- and be based on what is important to *others*: what will make us popular with them. If we do that, we're likely to base our behavior on what everyone else is doing, perhaps without even stopping to think about whether it's right or wrong. After all, how wrong can something be if everyone else is doing it?

But the fact that a lot of people are doing something doesn't mean it's right. In fact, what's *right* (i.e., *morally* right) is often just the opposite of what most people are doing, because too many people settle for what's *easiest* rather than what's *right*.

You can only build and reinforce a strong character by being true to yourself and to what *you* believe in, no matter what anyone else thinks or does. The decisions you make and the actions you take should be true to *your* character and based on *your* values. The more you stick to what you believe in, the more you'll reinforce those convictions.

While some may feel this discussion is mainly for young people -- those who are of an age where their value systems and character may still be developing -- that is definitely not my intention. Development and growth are not just for the young. Many people continue the process throughout their lives, which is what all of us should do: be constantly changing, strengthening our values, building character.

And there's no reason you can't do that, too, if you want to. The fact is, none of us are perfect, and few things are more satisfying than working toward becoming better at what you do and who you are.

Values

The dictionary defines a value as, "A principle, standard, or quality considered inherently worthwhile or desirable." Perhaps a more useful definition is, "A belief that one type of conduct is preferable to the opposite type of conduct." (Rokeach, 1973) Both definitions emphasize the fact that our values have a strong influence on our behavior by helping us distinguish right from wrong.

While some people have a clear sense of their values and are firmly committed to them, others don't seem to think much about values at all.

People with strong values take responsibility for their actions, take control over what they do, and influence what happens to them, while those without strong values are more likely to be influenced by what *other* people think and do.

Those with strong values know what they believe in, who they are, and what they stand for. Those without a clear sense of values, on the other hand, are likely to be influenced more by circumstances or by the philosophies of those around them -- philosophies like "if it feels good, do it" – rather than by any thought about what's right or wrong.

When you have a strong sense of your own values, you'll always have a frame of reference that you can use to determine when somebody else's values -- or the values of an organization -- don't agree with yours and then act accordingly.

Values give meaning to what we do. They influence our attitudes, shape our behaviors, are instrumental in which dreams and visions we pursue, and guide us in developing our personal plans for achieving our dreams. A strong value system and a positive, deliberately-developed character are the keys to personal credibility and a reputation you can be proud of.

Your values, along with your background and experience, are what define your unique character. Your character, in turn, guides your commitment to beliefs and values that are even larger than your own. Character influences how we do everything that we do: how we process information and make decisions, and how we interpret and manage the world around us.

Developing the kind of character you want requires a strong personal commitment, but once you've made that commitment, maintaining it will become easier and easier as your pride in the person you're becoming gets stronger and stronger.

Ethics

People of character not only let their values guide their decisions but also have a strong sense of responsibility to everyone who is, or will be, affected by their actions. Their decisions and actions are guided by *moral* standards -- not by convenience, opportunism, or self-interest.

A sense of responsibility is the foundation of *ethics*: the rules and standards that govern our conduct. Our personal codes of ethics are based on how willing we are to accept responsibility and accountability for our actions and to recognize and respect the rights of others.

Acting ethically sounds simple, and in principle, it is. But that doesn't mean it's *easy*. Living by our values is sometimes difficult, and the rewards aren't always immediate, but we do it because of our belief that it is the right way to live our lives.

Summary

Your character can have a major influence on your success or failure. You *will* develop some type of character whether you do it deliberately or just let it happen. But if you let it evolve on its own, it is much less likely to be an asset than if you make a conscious effort to develop the character you *want*.

Your character is based on the values that are most important to you: values that guide your behavior. Since it has a powerful influence on your behavior, character can be a strong deterrent to improper or unacceptable behavior. Your character defines your attitude and is a constant reminder of your values, beliefs, and responsibilities.

Good character is built on values like honesty, integrity, loyalty, and trust. We nurture and maintain character through our daily activities -- by constantly *practicing* what we believe in – and *our* actions can set a powerful example for others. In this sense, *what* we do and *how* we do it sends a much clearer message of our values and beliefs than anything we could possibly *say*.

> *"Sow a thought and you reap an act;*
> *Sow an act and you reap a habit;*
> *Sow a habit and you reap a character;*
> *Sow a character and you reap a destiny."*
> (Samuel Smiles, 1812-1904)

Organizations today are becoming more dependent on knowledge and less on manual labor. They expect the people they hire to take responsibility for their own actions: for how, where, and when they do their jobs.

As a result, they hire people they can depend on; people they can trust; people with character. They no longer try to control *how* people work as closely as they once did. They depend instead on the values, beliefs, and understood practices of people of good character.

Make sure you're one of *those* people.

Note: Portions of this chapter have been excerpted from *If Not Now, When?* (O'Neal, 2008: Chapter 14)

Don O'Neal

5. CREDIBILITY

*"When the one great scorer comes
to write against your name,
he marks – not that you won or lost –
but how you played the game."*
(Grantland Rice, 1880-1954)

While character is the foundation of personal integrity, our credibility is what gains the trust of others. Defined as, "believability; trustworthiness; reliability," a person's credibility is a function of his trustworthiness, consistency, and self-awareness.

Trustworthiness

Trust is defined as "confident belief; faith," which helps explain why we tend to trust those in whom we have confidence. But how does one gain that confidence and trust? What's it based on?

It's widely believed that we trust people who are predictable, which means trust cannot be mandated or purchased; it must be earned. (Bennis, Nanus, 1985:44,45) That being the case, we can't expect people to trust us simply because we *want* them to or because we *pay* them to. We earn trust through the reputation we build through what we do and how we do it.

We earn it by the depth of our commitment to a vision – to the things we believe in, by the sacrifices we make in pursuit of that vision, and by sticking to our values and principles regardless of the difficulties we encounter.

We earn trust by taking the *high* road rather than the easy way. We earn it by always doing what's *right*, rather than what's most popular. We earn it by the example we set -- by *living* our values and principles, not just voicing them.

Finally, we earn trust by first trusting others: giving them the benefit of the doubt. Of course there's some risk in trusting others first, but we take that risk knowing that our confidence in others will help them build confidence in themselves.

Consistency

A key element in credibility is consistency. Defined as "uniformity," being consistent makes us *predictable* in the eyes of others, and allows them to anticipate how we'll behave in any situation. And the more confident people are in how we'll behave, the more likely they are to trust us. They'll have more confidence in our decisions, even when they don't agree with them. Here's a personal example of the effect of one person's lack of consistency:

This was an executive who seemed to be two different people. One day he would cheerfully greet everyone he met, taking a genuine interest in each person. The next day he was just as likely to stride down the hall, passing everyone without smiling, without greeting, without speaking, without even making eye contact.

Working for him, I learned to quickly assess which person he might be on any given day. So any time I needed to consult with him, I would start our conversation with some small talk, like the weather, baseball, or something like that, so I could determine which personality he was wearing that particular day.

If it looked to be one of his "approachable" days, I would discuss whatever it was that I needed to talk with him about. But if it seemed to be one of his "out-of-it" days, I knew he would probably be much less receptive to an open discussion, so I'd make an early exit and come back another time.

Using that approach, we were able to establish a good working relationship, and I developed a great deal of respect for him both as an executive and as a person. In fact, I came to trust him.

Regrettably, those who didn't work with him on a day-to-day basis weren't able to develop a similar relationship, or any degree of trust, because of his inconsistency – his unpredictability. After all, how much can you trust a person when you have no idea how he might respond to you?

Unfortunately, his inconsistency made him untrustworthy in the eyes of many people. As a result, this extremely capable executive was much less effective than he might otherwise have been.

Self-Awareness

"To act with integrity, you must first know who you are. You must know what you stand for, what you believe in, and what you care most about." (Kouzes and Posner, 2007:50)

Self-awareness means getting to know yourself objectively and unemotionally. Although difficult and sometimes humbling, it's absolutely essential to self-development. Getting an accurate picture of who you are and how you operate requires an in-depth examination of your goals/expectations, capabilities, strengths, resources, and attitude.

Your strengths are the things you do *best* -- usually knowledge, skills, and abilities -- although some of your greatest strengths may also be your personal values, character, and reputation. It's important to have a clear idea of what are your real strengths so you can focus your attention on them.

But assessing your strengths may not be easy, because it's hard to be objective about yourself. Nevertheless, the best place to begin is with your own opinion, since you know yourself better than does anyone else.

Begin by listing the things at which you feel you're most competent, which will probably include the things you *like* best, that *interest* you the most, or at which you've been most *successful*.

Next, get opinions from others, since they can often see things about you that you can't. Which others? Anyone who *expect*s something of you or who is *affected* by what you do. That usually includes at least family, friends, and business associates.

They are constantly observing what you do, how well you do it, and how well you're meeting *their* expectations. Ask them to point out what they feel are your best points, your personal assets, your strengths.

Of course, there are those people who don't think they have *any* strengths. Theirs is a different kind of problem. Although *everyone* has strengths of one kind or another, they're not always obvious to us. But the fact they aren't obvious doesn't mean they don't have a special talent, or something that can be developed into a strength.

If you think this might be you -- if you're not sure if you *have* any strengths or are not sure what they are – asking others may be reassuring because they will often see strengths that aren't obvious to you.

Before you can expect to lead others effectively, and even before you can expect to be successful as an individual, you'll need to become the kind of person others will want to hire, work with, or be lead by. Self-development requires first becoming totally aware of yourself, then taking personal responsibility for yourself and your development.

Self-awareness puts you in touch with yourself. It helps you know yourself, including your goals and expectations, your capabilities, your strengths, the resources you have available ,and perhaps most important, your attitude.

Our discussion of self-awareness is consistent with what Bennis and Nanus describe as *positive self-regard*: "knowledge of one's strengths, the capacity to nurture and develop those strengths, and the ability to discern the fit between one's strengths and weaknesses and the organization's needs." (1985: 61, 62) In other words, objective awareness of your own strengths and weaknesses will help you apply your abilities in areas that meet both your own needs and those of any organization.

The more effectively you do that, the more likely you will be to enjoy the satisfaction of doing something you enjoy, can be proud of, and might be able to use to achieve success in your career.

Summary

Credibility is believability and is the basis of your reputation: what others think of you -- whether they hold you in high esteem or think little of you. One of the highest and most beneficial testimonials to anybody's trustworthiness is when someone says about you, "If he says so, you can bank on it."

Speaking of reputation, it's important never to forget how fragile a reputation can be and how much easier it is to lose a reputation than it is to build one or how easily you can damage another person's reputation, as the following example illustrates:

"According to an old fable, a young man told his confessor that he had damaged the reputation of another person in the village. The confessor ordered the man, as part of his penance, to go to the nearest hill and empty a bag of feathers to the wind.

After he had done so, scattering the feathers far and wide, the confessor told him to gather up all the feathers again. 'Gather them all! Impossible!' cried the young man. 'So too with the reputation you have damaged.' replied the confessor. 'I can give you absolution, but I doubt that you will ever be able to correct what you have done.'" (Hayes, 1983: 116)

Research has shown that more than anything, people want to follow leaders who are credible. *"Credibility is the foundation of leadership.* Above all else, we as constituents must be able to believe in our leaders.

We must believe that their word can be trusted, that they're personally passionate and enthusiastic about the work that they're doing, and that they have the knowledge and skill to lead." (Kouzes, Posner, 2007:37)

Here are five simple rules for ensuring your credibility:

1. Always tell the truth.

2. Always keep your promises.

3. Always admit your mistakes. Don't be afraid to say, "I was wrong."

4. When you don't know something don't be afraid to say, "I don't know."

5. Always give the benefit of the doubt, until evidence proves otherwise.

(Hayes, 1983:16-17)

As true as they are, is there anything in those rules that we didn't learn from our parents even before we started kindergarten?

6. ATTITUDE

*"Nothing great was ever achieved
without enthusiasm."*
Ralph Waldo Emerson, 1803-1882)

What exactly do we mean by attitude?

"A position of the body or manner of carrying oneself, indicative of a mood or condition. A state of mind or feeling with regard to a person or thing."

This, the dictionary definition, is open to interpretation. Based on it, attitude can be viewed in a number of different ways. It can mean how we present ourselves, how we feel about ourselves, or how we feel about another person or thing, to name just three.

But however we interpret it, attitude is up to the individual. How you feel about yourself affects how you present yourself, which in turn affects how you feel about others and how they feel about you.

Your attitude influences what you do, how you do it, and how effective you are. When you feel good about yourself, it shows in your enthusiasm, in the quality of your life, and in your relationships with others.

Your attitude can be a big advantage or can put you at a huge disadvantage, and it's completely within your control. In fact, you're the only one who *can* control your attitude, and it's important that you *do* control it, because it *will* affect your career and your life.

In fact, attitude is so important that many employers today consider it the single most important personal characteristic when they make hiring decisions. They realize that people can be taught the necessary skills and abilities for almost any job but that it's nearly impossible to change a person's attitude.

Of course, when we talk about controlling your attitude, we mean making sure you have a *positive* attitude. And that means a positive attitude in the eyes of others – in the eyes of those who are important to you, your career, and your life.

It should be comforting to note that attitude isn't something you were born with, nor are you stuck with the attitude you now have, whatever it is. Your attitude is *how you think*, and it's a choice. It can be whatever you want it to be; it's all up to you. How does one go about developing a positive attitude? You can begin by examining how you think about the things that influence attitude.

How You Think

Some of the most important elements that make up attitude are *dignity*, *dependability*, *work ethic*, *loyalty*, *respect*, *confidence*, *modesty*, *enthusiasm*, and *optimism*. Although each of them can have either positive or negative aspects, the following definitions are associated with a *positive* attitude.

Dignity
Dignity comes from your personal honor, grace, and self-esteem, and is what makes you worthy of the respect of others. Do you conduct yourself with dignity in the way you dress, act, and treat others?

Dependability
Dependability is measured by how conscientious, responsible, and reliable others believe you are. Are you seen as "a man of your word" when it comes to following through on your commitments, such as doing what you say you'll do, and being where you say you'll be, *when* you say you'll be there?

Work Ethic
Your work ethic is how diligently you execute your responsibilities in terms of the quantity, quality, and timeliness of what you do regardless of whether or not you are being watched. Do you do

your best and work your hardest all the time, or do you only do what you *have* to do?
"It is wretched taste to be gratified with mediocrity when the excellent lies before us."
(Isaac Disraeli, 1766-1848)

Loyalty
Loyalty is a measure of your allegiance to others - how faithful and steadfast you are to them. Are you true to others through the bad times as well as the good?

Respect
Respect is the esteem and regard you have for others and how considerate you are in your actions toward them. Do you treat others as you would like to be treated regardless of any differences you may have?

Confidence
Confidence is your self-reliance and is based on your self-assurance and how secure you are in yourself and your abilities. Do you believe in yourself and your abilities, or are you constantly questioning yourself?

Modesty
Modesty is a measure of your humility and unpretentiousness and may be the best defense against arrogance. Are you one who "toots your own horn," or do you share your accomplishments with others?

Enthusiasm

Enthusiasm is a measure of your interest, spirit, and excitement in or for something. Are you usually excited about the things in which you're involved, or do you see them as just something else to put up with?

Optimism

Optimism is the ability or willingness to see the positive side of any situation, to expect the best outcome, or see the most hopeful aspects. Do you face each day and each assignment as a new opportunity or as just another obstacle to overcome?

Overall, an attitude that suggests you care only about yourself isn't likely to enhance your integrity in the eyes of others. Although your own needs are important, they aren't the *only* needs you should think about. You should make sure you understand the needs of the people who are important to you, including your family, friends, and those with whom you work closely.

Self-Discipline

Do you have times when you wish you had nothing to do, when you could just sit back and let things happen? Me too. In fact, most of us do have times we feel as though it would be so much easier if we didn't have to make an effort to do anything at all.

But deep down most of us realize that our future will turn out better if we plan how we want it to be, then do whatever it takes to make it happen that way. And that's why we willingly give up some of the things we want today for a better tomorrow.

Focusing on the future requires the self-discipline to take responsibility for ourselves and for our actions. When we do that, we're saying, "My life will be what *I* make of it, not what circumstances, or someone else, makes of it."

People who are self-disciplined help ensure their future success by developing good habits, like being organized, arriving on time, being dependable and consistent, and making the best use of their time and efforts.

They accept responsibility for their failures as well as their successes. And when things go wrong, they don't blame it on someone else or on bad luck; they accept full responsibility for the consequences of their actions.

Self-discipline is what helps us make the *right* choices rather than taking the *easy* way out.

Satisfaction

Research has shown a direct connection between employee satisfaction and customer satisfaction and between customer satisfaction and the success of any organization. In other words, the more satisfied a company's employees are, the better they will satisfy customers. And the more satisfied the customers are, the more successful the firm will be.

Translating that to a more personal level, your own level of satisfaction will have a lot to do with your attitude and enthusiasm, which in turn will affect how you come across to others.

When those others are people who can affect your future success, your attitude will directly affect the impression they have of you -- how *satisfied* they are with you -- and can ultimately have a direct bearing on *your* success.

Where does personal satisfaction come from? Largely from how we feel about ourselves. Do we feel good about who we are, how we're doing, *what* we're doing? Or do we feel frustrated, dissatisfied, discontent, unsuccessful?

When we feel good about ourselves, it shows in our attitude, our enthusiasm, the quality of our lives, and in how we come across to others.

So personal satisfaction can be either a big advantage or a major disadvantage both in our relationships with others and in our lives. After all, don't you find it more enjoyable to be around someone who is positive and upbeat rather than someone who always seems to be downtrodden and demoralized?

That's why your attitude – how you think and how you feel about yourself - can have such a powerful influence on how successful you are in realizing your dreams and achieving your goals.

When you feel you're making progress, it motivates you to do whatever it takes to keep going.

On the other hand, anytime you feel like you're just spinning your wheels, it can be discouraging, de-motivating, and can make you start thinking: "I'll never get there, so why try?"

So motivation is a critical element, not just in your personal satisfaction but also in maintaining a positive attitude.

Motivation

Everything we desire is driven by some *need* or *want*. We want it because it will *do* something for us or give us satisfaction or for how it will make us feel. The desire to satisfy those needs -- or to get what we want -- is perhaps our most powerful motivator.

We hear a lot about motivation: "She's motivated." "He's not motivated." Then there's the "motivated seller," a catch-phrase in real estate, meaning that the owner of a property has a strong desire or need to sell it. There are two basic sources of motivation: external (extrinsic) and internal (intrinsic.)

External motivation "pushes" people to do what *someone else* wants done, and they do it -- not because they *want* to -- but to get a reward. They know, of course, that if they don't do it they won't be rewarded.

This is often referred to as the "carrot and stick" method, and is based on the theory that you could get a mule to move forward by tying a carrot to the end of a long stick and holding it out in front of him. The mule will supposedly walk forward, thinking he'll get the carrot.

Internal motivation, on the other hand, "pulls" a person to do something because that person *wants* to do it either to satisfy himself or to please someone else. Here, the reward is in the doing. It comes from the personal satisfaction, the sense of accomplishment. In effect, we reward *ourselves*, and the only potential for punishment is the disappointment if we don't succeed.

Which is best, most effective? The research is quite clear: internal motivation is much more effective than external. Nobody can motivate us as well as we can motivate ourselves.

Successful people, for example, are usually highly self-motivated: they want what they desire so badly they'll do whatever it takes to get it. And that applies to most of us: if we want something badly enough, we may be willing to do whatever is necessary to get it. But we aren't likely to be nearly as motivated if *someone else* wants us to do something.

The only way someone else can get us to do what *they* want is by finding a way to make us *want* to do it. That means the only time most of us are willing to do something for someone else is when we ourselves will benefit in some way. In other words, we are most likely to take action when it will have some personal benefit.

In that sense, we're all driven to some degree by the unspoken question, "What's in it for me?" -- a question that's a primary driver of motivation.

Summary

Your attitude is an indicator of how you view the world: it reflects whether you're optimistic or pessimistic, enthusiastic or bored, independent or dependent, confident or wary, dependable or unpredictable, and respectful or disrespectful.

Your attitude isn't only how you feel about yourself, but more importantly, how others will feel about you. It wl affect everything you do and everyone you touch either in a positive or negative way. And it's all up to you.

It's you who can choose *how you think.*

It's you who can develop the *self-discipline* that will guide you in making the *right* choices instead of the easy ones.

And the right attitude and self-discipline are what will ultimately bring you the greatest *satisfaction* from your efforts and accomplishments and provide the internal *motivation* that will enable you to do whatever it takes to meet your most cherished needs.

Note: Portions of this chapter have been excerpted from *If Not Now, When?* (O'Neal,2008 Chapter 3) and *Developing Leaders* (O'Neal, 2009: Chapters 5 and 13.)

PART III –

RESPONSIBILITY

Responsibility means accountability; dependability; reliability; trustworthiness; and involves important duties or obligations. (American Heritage Dictionary)

Any discussion of responsibility, or accountability, begs the questions: "Responsible to *whom*?"; "Accountable to *whom*?"; and, "For *what favor*?" The answers, of course, depend on the individual: who you are and what you believe. You may see yourself as responsible to:

- God,
- Yourself,
- Mankind, or the human race,
- Those who look to you
  as an example.

Those who believe they are here on earth for a purpose are likely to think first of their responsibility to God, their creator.

I, for one, believe we are all indebted to our creator for the gift of *life*. We were granted life on earth not as a sentence to be served but as an opportunity to *do* something, to *change* something, to make something *better.*

We are *not* here simply to get by -- to endure. We're here to make the world a better place -- to leave it better than we found it. Our responsibility isn't merely to survive; it's to thrive and to help others thrive.

While some may not accept this view of life, it will come naturally to those of you who have children, because the major responsibilities of parenthood include protecting our children, seeing that they get the most out of life, helping them have a good life.

There are, however, those who define a *good* life as "more." They may work at more than one job so they can have more, and give their children more, where *more* means more possessions. Unfortunately, living life that way is likely to deprive their children of things that are much more important than possessions: their parents' time, attention, love, and affection.

The chapters in this section discuss the fundamentals of our responsibility to others: *duty, respect, understanding,* and *example.*

PART III – RESPONSIBILITY (to *others*)

Chapter 7 – DUTY
            Obligation
            Unselfishness

Chapter 8 – RESPECT
            Trust
            Expectations

Chapter 9 – COMMUNICATION
            Understanding
            Empathy
            Questioning

Chapter 10 – EXAMPLE
            Role-Modeling
            Encouragement

Don O'Neal

7. DUTY

"No man is an island, entire of itself;
every man is a piece of the continent,
a part of the main"
         (John Donne, 1572-1631)

The dictionary defines duty as, "An act or a course of action that one should or must do. A moral obligation."

We all have duties, moral obligations. Some we were born with; others we accumulate as we go through life. Doing our duty as individuals requires acknowledging that we have *obligations*, identifying what they are, and to whom, then *unselfishly* taking whatever actions are necessary to meet those obligations.

Obligation

Throughout our lives, we all need help from others from time to time to overcome obstacles and challenges we face. As a result, we are obligated to various people and groups of people -- for example, our parents -- for all they've done for us.

Don O'Neal

While it's hard to imagine how anyone could get through life entirely on their own, there are those who feel they have done it all *themselves* so they don't owe anything to anybody. Some even complain, "I didn't ask to be born," and feel their parents are obligated to *them* -- part of a misguided philosophy that parents have a responsibility to make their children's lives as easy as possible.

Anyone who thinks like that probably has little sense of responsibility or duty. Hopefully, they are only a small percentage of us, but if you happen to be one of them, you might as well stop reading right now and give this book to someone who will get some good from it. It certainly isn't for you.

Those of you who may have been shocked by that seemingly rude outburst but are still with me may sense that this is one of my soapbox issues, and you'd be right! In my opinion, one of today's major societal problems is the number of people who refuse to take responsibility for themselves -- who believe everything that happens to them is someone else's fault, never the result of their own actions or inaction.

But hopefully there's a majority of us who recognize that being born is a priceless gift that comes with serious obligations. To name just a few, we owe our creator for the gift of life; our parents for making it possible for us to be born and nurturing us through infancy and childhood; and all who helped provide the knowledge, skills, and abilities that give us the opportunity to live meaningful lives.

How can we ever repay them? It's simple. By striving to become the best person you can be. Do that, and you'll have the personal satisfaction of knowing that not only are you repaying your obligations, you're making the world around you a bit better in the process. It is a fact that the more unselfish you are, the more you benefit from your own generosity.

Unselfishness

Most of us were taught two principles early in life: to *treat others as we would like to be treated,* and to *share*. These principles are the foundation of unselfishness. Perhaps that's why childhood is often cited as the most generous time of our lives. But for some reason, that seems to change as we grow older; we seem to forget those principles. Why is that?

I believe it has a lot to do with competition. Although children would rather cooperate than compete, "our schooling, from the earliest grades, trains us not only to triumph over others but to regard them as obstacles to our success." (Kohn, 1986:2)

That may be because so many schools grade students with a quota system that's based on the philosophy that the majority of students (perhaps 60-80 percent) should be graded as "average," a few (perhaps 10-20 percent) as "below average," and a few (perhaps 10-20 percent) as "above average." That means a class of 20 students would have 1 or 2 getting A's, 1 or 2 receiving D's or F's, and the remaining 16 to 18 getting B's or C's.

Unfortunately, limiting the number of A's automatically puts students in competition for grades, which means they will have little incentive to cooperate. After all, "Why should I help someone else get a good grade if it lowers my chance for one?"

That's in direct conflict with what parents teach their children about unselfishness; it teaches them the exact opposite -- to think only about themselves.

And competition seems to intensify as we get older. In elementary school, it's for grades; in high school, for admission to college; in college, for grade-point average; and after college, for jobs, performance evaluations, and promotion. And of course, there's athletic competition, which now begins well before school-age.

Some argue that competition is a necessary part of life, and therefore, inevitable. Fortunately not everyone agrees. It's been my experience that in many situations in school and in life, *cooperation* is much more effective than competition. That's because competition pushes people to triumph over *others*, while cooperation encourages us to triumph over *ourselves* – to be the best we can be.

That's why schools that use non-competitive grading based on measurable standards for what students must do to earn an A or B or C, etc., have proven much more effective in terms of learning outcomes. Each student's work is measured against the same standard, and he or she is given the grade she earns based only on the standard, not the grades of other students.

This creates an environment in which students learn more, and they learn from each other -- not to mention the fact that it reinforces what their parents have taught them about unselfishness. Unfortunately, this system is not as widely used as the competitive form.

Now let's shift our attention from the schoolroom to the workplace. In many organizations, performance evaluation largely ignores what a person has done well, focusing instead on finding fault. And some companies actually increase competition among employees by comparing workers with each other, much like schools grade students. And like teachers, managers are required to evaluate the majority of people as "good," a small percentage as "excellent," and another small percentage as "poor."

Now, think about it: is it realistic to expect people to be unselfish, to be team-players, when they are forced to compete with one another? Of course not! It simply doesn't work. When we're engaged in competition, our survival instincts warn us that if we help them, it will hurt our own chances.

But if we measure people against a standard instead of each other, their focus will be on *self-improvement,* and there is no single winner, and no losers, because everyone has the same opportunity to succeed.

So what does all of this mean? First, meeting our obligations requires unselfishness. We each have a personal responsibility to do what is right, no matter what it takes, regardless of what anyone else does. Second, competition can be the enemy of unselfishness, but cooperation is its friend.

Those interested in leadership should recognize that among those you lead, unselfishness can make the difference between success and failure, which means providing incentives for cooperation is essential. Any system that puts individuals in competition with one another will destroy whatever desire they may have to work as a team.

Summary

One of the best examples of duty for those of us who are fortunate to live in a free republic like the United States of America is our obligation to preserve that freedom and pass it on to future generations. The basis of our society is government "of the people, by the people, for the people..." (Lincoln's Gettysburg Address), which means our government is totally dependent upon the citizens of the United States.

As citizens, this means we have a duty to support our country's legal system, its legislative system, and its system of justice. Fulfilling that duty requires us to obey the laws of the land, vote for those who run for public office or run for office ourselves, and serve on juries when called to do so.

These are fundamental obligations that we accept as responsibilities of citizenship, and the effectiveness of our society depends on the participation of every citizen in carrying out these essential duties.

In addition to our duty as citizens, we have a duty is to do whatever it takes to meet our obligations to others, not just because we *feel* obligated, but because it's the *right thing to do*. But it's important to understand that doing the right thing is seldom the *easiest* path. It will often require a deep sense of unselfishness and a commitment to the idea that the best way to repay our obligations is to make the most or our lives.

And never forget the power of *cooperation*. In his book, *Nonzero: The Logic of Human Destiny*, Robert Wright makes a compelling argument that over the course of human history, advances in technological innovation and improvement in the quality of human life have come about much more through cooperation than through competition.

Although the unselfishness required to do your duty may sometimes require sacrificing your self-interests for the greater good, the satisfaction that comes from knowing you've done the right thing may be the closest any of us will ever come to true happiness.

"I don't know what your destiny will be, but one thing I know; the only ones among you who will be really happy are those who have sought and found how to serve."

Albert Schweitzer, 1875-1965)

Don O'Neal

8. RESPECT

"...so to love wisdom
as to live accordingly to its dictates,
a life of simplicity, independence,
magnanimity, and trust."
(Henry David Thoreau, 1817-1862)

In Chapter 6 we discussed *respect* as an important element of attitude: "Respect is the esteem and regard we have for others, and how considerate we are in our actions toward them." Now we need to examine why we respect some people and not others.

Our respect for someone else may be based on that person's accomplishments, on the opinion of someone we trust, or on personal experience, but it can also be influenced by how we feel about people in general.

For example, a cynical person may have difficulty respecting *anyone*, while someone with a high opinion of people in general may find it easy. Most of us probably fall somewhere in between; our natural tendency may be to *like* people, but just one bad experience can make us suspicious, particularly of someone who has disappointed us in some way.

My own approach is to give everyone the benefit of the doubt when I first meet them, and leave it to them to justify my respect or to lose it. I begin with high expectations and trust that people will meet them, but if they don't, my opinion of them and respect for them will suffer.

Now that we've discussed some of the things that influence our respect *for* others, let's turn our attention to what you as an individual can do to gain the respect *of* others.

All you have to do is be *worthy* of respect. It's really that simple, but being simple doesn't mean it's easy. Respect doesn't come automatically; it has to be *earned* by what you do and how you do it. It's all about t*rust* and *expectations*.

Trust

The dictionary defines trust as "The condition and resulting obligation of having confidence placed in one."

Other people will only have confidence in you when they believe you will live up to their expectations. So their confidence gives you an obligation to do everything you can to justify their trust.

But your obligation isn't only to them; you also have one to *yourself* -- an obligation to set high expectations for yourself and to strive to become the best that you can be.

Expectations

The foundation of your expectations should be your *vision*: your plan for where you want to go, why you want to get there, and what kind of person you want to become. So you must make sure your vision is inspirational enough to lift your expectations high, because we seldom exceed our own expectations. Your vision should be so challenging it stretches your imagination, your expectations, and your efforts to achieve those expectations.

The higher you aim the farther you'll go, and you don't need exceptional skills or knowledge to reach high goals. All it takes is dedication and hard work, and by hard work I don't mean you need to be a slave to your job; all you have to do is just a bit more than the average person.

That means committing yourself to getting every task done in a timely manner and working to the best of your ability, every time. You don't have to be a genius; you just have to do your *best* in every situation, as I learned early in my career:

When I told him I had accepted a job with a large company, a friend remarked, "That company has thousands of employees; aren't you afraid you'll be just a *number*?"

This was my first real job after college -- all of my work experience had been for individuals and small businesses, in summer jobs -- so I didn't have a good response.

But it didn't take me long to learn that, although many people in large organizations *do* feel like they're just numbers, they don't *have* to feel that way. I soon realized that how I feel about myself and my work is entirely up to me; it doesn't have to depend on the organization. I found I could stand out, even in that big company, by believing in myself and having high expectations.

The bigger the organization, the more people there are who are content doing the minimum that's expected of them, thereby allowing a willing worker with high expectations to stand out, and I did. Within just a few months, I had earned a reputation as a person who always got the job done and did it well.

But my reputation wasn't just from working hard; it was also because I was willing to do *anything* I was assigned, even those lousy jobs everyone else tried hard to avoid. Whatever the assignment, I gave it my best, and it wasn't long before I started getting better projects. Why? Because my manager trusted me; he had confidence that I would always do my best. I had earned his respect.

Although that may not sound like an earth-shaking discovery – the value of working hard and doing everything I was assigned to the best of my ability – it turned out to be one of the most valuable lessons I ever learned and has had an enormous influence on my career in every organization I've worked for.

And that company wasn't unusual; I've found the same thing to be true in every large organization I've worked with. Workers typically set their expectations by watching their peers work and trying to keep pace with them. That can be a good thing if the pace-setters are the kind of workers whose examples inspire their co-workers.

But too often there seems to be an unwritten understanding that nobody will work hard enough to make anyone else look bad by comparison. When that's the culture in an organization, those trying to work hard will soon get the message, spoken or unspoken, "slow down, you're making the rest of us look bad," and the pace of work will level off at the slowest rate that's acceptable to management.

That not only damages the organization, but also the careers, reputations, and job security of everyone who works there. So, should you ever find yourself in that kind of environment, remember, you have a clear choice: become one of the many who are content to do average work or one of the few who won't settle for anything less than their best.

While going along with the crowd (not making waves) may be easier, more comfortable, and less of a hassle, it is *never* the road to personal success. Pride, satisfaction, and success only come from setting high standards for yourself and striving to be better than just "good enough." But choosing to excel will never be an easy path, because you won't be popular with those who are afraid you might make them look bad.

So, if the way you work upsets those around you, remind them it's *their* problem, not yours, and keep on doing your best. Giving in to the fears of others may be the easiest path, but it will make *you* the loser, and you won't be the only one; your employer and your family will suffer, too.

You'll be sacrificing your reputation and your dreams, for what? What will you get for what you're giving up? Perhaps you'll get back in their good graces, but will it be *worth* it? Always remember, working harder or smarter than someone else won't put them at a disadvantage unless they *let* it; unless they're not willing to work as hard as you; unless they aren't willing to pay the same price.

The truth is, you're not trying to be better than anyone else, because you aren't competing with *them*. You're only competing with *yourself,* and they have the same opportunity.

Whenever you excel -- and you *will* excel -- don't expect everyone to give you credit for what you've accomplished. It will be too painful for some people to applaud your success, and they're likely to say it's only because you're lucky, even though you may have worked and sacrificed for years to accomplish what you have.

You will never be able to please everyone, so make sure you're satisfied with yourself before you worry about what others will think.

Although my last example took place in a career setting, I believe that its concepts – and all of the concepts in this book – can be applied in any area of your life that you choose.

Which leads me to one final thought on personal expectations. It's interesting, when you think about it, how some people have completely different expectations for their work than for their hobbies. At their jobs, they may be content to work at the same pace as everyone else, but they have entirely different expectations when working on something for themselves.

That may be because when we're doing something *we* want to do (e.g., woodworking, art, gardening, traveling), we have high expectations. After all, it's our *own* project, and our self-respect is at stake. We get personal satisfaction from doing our best, but it hurts our pride if it isn't done well.

Now, as you might imagine, this is a soapbox issue for me. There is absolutely no reason we shouldn't work to those same high standards when we're working for someone else. Remember, the company you work for is *not* your enemy; it's your source of income -- your bread and butter.

And your paycheck comes with an obligation to help your company succeed. If it fails, it's your job that's at stake. So whatever you do, *never* lower your personal expectations, whether you're working for yourself or for someone else. Tell yourself something like this:

"I owe it to myself, and to my self-esteem and self-confidence, to always do my best, even when I know it may not be appreciated by others. I can take comfort in the knowledge that *I* appreciate it, and in the final analysis, my opinion is what really matters."

You'll benefit from high expectations in at least two ways: the satisfaction you'll get from achieving what you set out to do, and the pride that comes from knowing you did your best.

A final note: Remember, you have two sets of obligations – to yourself, and to others (your employer, for example) – so you'll have two sets of questions to consider when setting your expectations:

"What are my expectations for *myself*, and what will I need to do to meet them?"

"Who *else's* expectations should I be trying to meet, and what will I need to do to meet them?"

Summary

The best way to earn the respect of others is by being the kind of person they can trust, and you do that by always meeting your obligations.

The expectations we set for ourselves become our personal standards of performance, so to be an above-average performer, you have to set above-average expectations. But why try to excel? What's in it for you?

The benefits should be self-evident: pride, self-esteem, and the satisfaction you'll get from doing good work. You'll feel better about yourself and everything you do, and your reputation, career, and life will all be enriched.

Aiming high -- setting high expectations for yourself -- can be one of the most powerful tools you'll ever find to assist you in your life, your career, and in reaching your dreams.

You owe it to yourself to be better than just *good* at whatever you do; to always try to be the best that you can be. That's the way to earn self-respect and the respect of others.

Don O'Neal

9. COMMUNICATION

"If you want to understand others,
look into your own heart."
(Johann Friedrich von Schiller, 1759-1805)

Although communication requires at least two people -- one to send a message, and one to receive it -- most of the time we seem to focus on the sender's point of view. "How can I get my message across to my target audience? How can I make sure they hear my message, or see it?"

But if we want to answer those questions, we also have to know something about our intended receivers.

It's important to remember that we as individuals are all different. So when more than one person hears or sees a presentation or discussion, each will form his or her own interpretation, and every person's interpretation is likely to be different. Everything you and I see and hear is filtered through our own experience, and since our experiences are different, it's unlikely we'll both have the same understanding.

That means no matter how clear we feel our message is being sent, it will never be as clear to our receivers as it is to us, which is why *understanding* is so critical to effective communication.

Understanding

How well receivers understand a message depends on two things: how effectively the sender transmits her intentions, and how well receivers interpret what she means.

So to deliver a message that will be clearly understood, the sender will have to think like the receiver: "If I were in his/her shoes, what would get my attention?" You not only have to know who your receivers are but also what is most meaningful and significant to them as individuals. People will be more likely to "get" your message if it appeals in some personal way to their needs, wants, desires, or interests.

But clarifying the message isn't just the responsibility of the sender; it's also up to the receiver. The best communication occurs when the receiver has a sincere *desire* to understand what the sender means, which means if the receiver doesn't try to understand the message from the sender's point of view, he isn't likely to get the true meaning.

So effective communication depends as much on the receiver *wanting* to understand what the sender is trying to say as on how well the sender understands the receiver. The degree of that understanding depends on *empathy*, on the part of the sender – a desire to understand what's important to the receiver – and the receiver – a desire to understand the sender's intentions. What's the secret to developing that level of understanding? It has a lot to do with *how* the message is delivered.

Research has shown that approximately 55 percent of the *meaning* of any conversation is transmitted by facial expression and body language, and 38 percent through voice inflection. (Wellner, 2005:37-38)

That means if the people we're communicating with cannot see us or hear us, they are likely to miss as much as 93 percent of our meaning, since only about 7 percent of it is transmitted by words alone. Considering how important understanding is to effective communication, is 7 percent understanding enough to get our message across? Not likely.

With that in mind, think about how well the messages you send by e-mail, text messaging, memos, letters, and faxes are likely to come across to your receivers. Think about the huge gap in understanding they're likely to leave. Phone conversations are somewhat better, as they capture both the words (7 percent) and voice inflection (38 percent), but they still leave 55 percent of the meaning subject to misunderstanding.

That means if we want to make sure our receivers understand what we're trying to say, face-to-face communication is far better than any other form of communication. It also means we should limit written and electronic communication to *factual* information, never anything that's emotional or that can be misunderstood.

But there is a place for written communication. In face-to-face and phone conversations, we sometimes respond on the spur of the moment with comments that we haven't had time to completely think through.

And later when we think back on the conversation, we often wish we'd responded differently. And the more urgent or spontaneous the discussion, the higher that risk. So when you're in a hurry, it might be a good idea to put off responding until you've had time to think about it, and then respond in writing.

Written communication can allow us to take time to think about the circumstances and possible consequences, write out a response, then revise it until we feel comfortable with it. That's particularly important if the conversation is emotional, or becomes heated.

When that happens, writing a response lets us express our thoughts, but only after we've had time to cool down so we can be more thoughtful and less emotional.

At one point in my business career, I became so frustrated with a situation in my company, I felt I was about to explode. Fortunately, instead of expressing myself verbally, I decided to write a letter to the CEO. After laboring over it to the point where I felt it was stating my concerns pretty well, I decided to get my boss's opinion before sending it on. After looking it over, he brought it back to me with just one comment: "This will be one of the best letters you never sent." He didn't have to say anything more to get his message across: "It's fine to get your frustrations down on paper, but you may have more to lose than gain by sending it."

After thinking about it overnight, I decided not to send the letter, and was later grateful for his advice.

It comes down to this: effective communication is making sure your audience understands what you're trying to say, and when *you* are the audience, making sure you do your best to understand what the sender is trying to say.

Empathy

Defined as, "trying to understand another person's feelings and motivations," empathy gives us insight into *why* people act the way they do and helps us better understand how they are likely to respond in different situations.

Sometimes we use communication to persuade someone else to *do* something – to get them to think, feel, purchase, vote, etc. If I want you to do something, it helps if I know what motivates you – what makes you take action. But without empathy, it may be impossible for me to understand your situation, your feelings, or your motives, so I will have difficulty determining what will get you to act the way I want you to.

By the same token, if you're the receiver and you don't have a sincere desire to *understand* what I'm trying to say, you're not likely to get my true meaning. And if you don't pay close *attention* to what I'm trying to say, you not only won't understand, but you'll be sending me a message that you don't really care.

Empathy means respecting another person's opinion whether you *like* the person or not. Without some degree of empathy, you're not likely to understand what someone else is trying to say.

Questioning

Questions can increase understanding in both directions: when used by a receiver to clarify the message, and when used by the sender, to get a feel for how effectively the message is being received or to more actively involve the receivers in the conversation.

Questions receivers might ask to improve their understanding include:

- This is what I heard you say -
             is it accurate?
- Could you repeat that?
- Does that mean....?

But you, as a *sender,* can also use questions to help you understand receivers' feelings and what is important to them, to encourage them to provide information, opinions, and ideas, and to help *them* understand your intentions.

Questioning stimulates involvement and helps make communication a circular process where we alternate between sending and receiving until there is clear understanding.

Summary

Communication is much more than just speaking and making presentations because it isn't just one way; it's a circular process beginning with someone sending a message and someone else receiving and trying to understand it, sometimes asking questions to help clarify and improve their understanding.

And remember, more than 90 percent of a conversation's meaning is conveyed through facial expression, body language, and voice inflection. And none of these are present in letters, email, or text messages.

Don O'Neal

10. EXAMPLE

"Example is not the main thing in life –
it is the only thing."
(Albert Schweitzer, 1875-1965)

"No man is so insignificant
as to be sure his example does no harm."
(Lord Clarendon, 1609-1674)

Are you a "people watcher"? I am some of the time, and I'll bet most of us are at one time or another. Why do we enjoy watching other people? Because we're all different, which makes us interesting, and it's also one way we form opinions about people: by watching what they do and how they do it.

Of course it works, both ways: while we're watching them, they're watching us. That means you and I are constantly on display, whether we want to be or not, even when we may not realize we're being watched. No matter who we are, where we are, or what we're doing, just about everything we do is likely to be seen by somebody.

"So what?" you might ask, "Who cares?"

Well, *you* should care, and *I* should care. We *all* should care because we are walking, talking *examples,* always displaying what kind of people we are to those around us.

That's why it's important that we carefully choose the kind of example we'd like to be. You can come across as someone who is rude, insensitive, undisciplined, arrogant, or even immoral, or you can behave in a way that people look up to, respect, admire.

Your *example* is what the rest of the world sees. It doesn't matter what you *say*, or what you *want* people to *think.* The only thing that counts is what they *see* because, in their eyes, the you they see is the *real* you.

You may not care how others see you, but you *should* care about how *you* see *yourself,* because that can have a major effect on your self-esteem. So whether you like it or not, you are a *role-model* for those around you, and for yourself.

Role-Modeling

As children, we are influenced by people who are older, like our parents, teachers, brothers and sisters, sports heroes, and movie stars. How do they influence us? What makes us look up to them? It might be respect, admiration, reputation, accomplishments, or simply their looks. Whatever it is, it makes them our role-models.

All parents hope our children will look up to people who are *good* examples, who will show, by their example, the right way to do things. But, unfortunately, that doesn't always happen because there are a lot of bad role-models out there -- some who are actually proud of the fact that they're "bad," and a lot more who *unintentionally* set bad examples by doing things on the sly that they think nobody will see.

So we're not just examples when we're *trying* to be; we're examples *all* of the time, by everything we do. Even when we think nobody can see what we're doing, there's a good chance somebody will. So we should always be conscious of what kind of example we're setting. Our personal example is one of the most visible ways we demonstrate our personal integrity and show others what kind of people we are.

Whether we intend to or not, in some sense, we're all leading some of the time by the examples we set. We may not think of ourselves as leaders, nor have any intention of leading others, but we're leader, nevertheless, though in a quiet way -- the same way some of our greatest leaders have led, more by their personal example than by any conscious attempt to inspire others.

Linus Torvalds is a good example of quiet leadership in the business world. The inventor of Linux, the world-wide open-source software development system, he "...presides over what may be the largest collaborative project in history. He holds no ownership rights beyond the name, no royalties and no authority over the tens of thousands of programmers who have worked on Linux. He has only influence."

(Executive Leadership, 2008:4)

Torvalds:
- surrounds himself with an informal circle of deputies
- treats each team member as an individual
- meets in person with his team at least once a year,
- admits his mistakes
- has a light touch
- avoids taking sides and splintering the group
- puts off making decisions when things turn messy, to let hotheads cool down

We should always be conscious of the example we're setting because at some point, the kind of people we are will affect those around us, especially our families, friends, and co-workers. Our example can either encourage and inspire them or disappoint and discourage them; the choice is ours and is a responsibility we should not take lightly.

By the same token, your personal example can be an ongoing inspiration for *yourself,* reinforcing what you believe in and the way you've chosen to live your life.

Encouragement

One of the most powerful ways of helping others is through encouragement. Consciously or unconsciously, we are constantly evaluating other people – what they do and how they do it -- and the way we use that information can either encourage or discourage them.

We can either criticize what they do wrong or praise what they do right, and which we choose usually has a lot to do with our attitude about people and life and whether we look at them positively or negatively.

Positive reinforcement is much more effective than criticism, whether we're talking about children or adults. When people are praised for what they do right, they invariably respond by doing more of what's right and less of what's wrong, because we all like being praised, and we all want to succeed.

Sometimes all it takes for people to succeed is more recognition for what they do *right* and less criticism for their failures -- more encouragement and less condemnation. And that's where your personal example can be a big help: when we encourage others, they are more likely to encourage those around them.

Summary

Setting the right example means practicing what we preach -- always doing what we say we will. An excellent recipe for becoming a good role model is the definition of *credibility* we discussed in Chapter 5:

- Honesty – always tell the truth,
- Trustworthiness – always keep your promises,
- Admit your mistakes,
- When you don't know something, say so,
- Always give the benefit of the doubt.

Anyone who aspires to lead others will surely find their own example to be a major factor in their success by either inspiring their followers or discouraging them. By the way she conducts herself, a good leader exemplifies the kinds of values, decisions, and actions that will earn the respect of followers. And it is ultimately the leader's personal credibility that earns the respect of followers and gives them confidence that following this leader and this vision will help them achieve the future they desire.

PART IV - OPPORTUNITY

An *opportunity* can be anything that looks like it might be an advantage, or make things easier for us, while a *threat* can be anything that looks as though it might be a problem, or make life more difficult. But most of the time, an opportunity and a threat are the same thing; the only difference is how we see them. How can something be both an opportunity and a threat?

It has a lot to do with the element of *surprise*. If we see something coming before it starts to affect us, we can do something to prepare for it, which makes it less of a surprise, less threatening, and might even give us time to turn it into an opportunity. But if we *didn't* see it coming, we'll be more likely to be taken by surprise, and see it as threatening.

Change is one of the major sources of opportunities and threats. While there are people who seem to see opportunity in almost any situation, unfortunately, there are many others who are so threatened by change and worry so much about how it might affect them that they only see the threats.

And that's understandable, because opportunities aren't always easy to recognize. They don't come clearly labeled, "here's an opportunity." On the contrary, they more often come cleverly disguised as problems, obstacles, or negative situations, so they don't *look like* opportunities; that is, until after we've seen someone else take advantage of them.

And even when we *do* see opportunities, we often let them pass by because they didn't come along at "the right time"; that is, they didn't appear at a time that was *convenient*. Well, in my experience, the best opportunities have always come along at the *worst* possible times -- at the most inconvenient times imaginable.

I'll provide some examples in the chapters that follow, chapters that discuss the essential elements of opportunity, including *foresight, focus, ability, action,* and *courage.*

11. FORESIGHT

"For I dipped into the future,
far as human eye could see,
saw the vision of the world,
and all the wonders that would be."
(Alfred, Lord Tennyson, 1809-1892)

"We should all be concerned
about the future because
we will have to spend
the rest of our lives there."
(Charles F. Kettering, 1876-1958)

Change

Because the world around us is constantly changing, it's important to watch *how* it's changing so we can be prepared for whatever it might bring. Anyone who isn't looking ahead is likely to be caught off guard when change starts to affect them.

How well we're prepared for change depends on foresight: whether we actively look for what's likely to happen in the future or only concern

Don O'Neal

ourselves with what's happening *now*. If we pay
attention to what's coming, we can see change as an
opportunity, but it can be a *threat* if it catches us
unaware.

An opportunity is "a good position, chance, or
prospect," while a threat is "an indication or
warning of probable trouble." Would you rather be
in "a good position," or "probable trouble"? I'll take
a good position over probable trouble any time, so
looking ahead for opportunities so I won't be faced
with threats later on seems like a no-brainer to me.

Looking Ahead

It's easy to spot an opportunity after it's gone --
anyone can do that -- but looking back only shows
what a good opportunity it *was*. That's why every
now and then we'll hear someone say, "I could have
bought that house 10 years ago for half of what it's
worth today," or something like that.

So past opportunities are gone, but what about
current opportunities -- those that are here *now?*
Unfortunately, they're almost as useless as past
opportunities because by the time they're here,
someone else will most likely have taken advantage
of them.

If *past* opportunities are gone and the value of
current opportunities has probably been siphoned
off by the time we see them, our best hope is to look
for *future* opportunities. And we need to spot them
far in advance while there's still time to do

something about them. While that may sound difficult, it isn't.

We can spot future opportunities by looking for *trends* – things just starting to happen that might affect us sometime in the future -- but we have to see them while they're still developing.

Timing is important because if we don't see a trend well in advance -- before it starts affecting us -- it's likely to become more of a threat than an opportunity.

Seeing a trend while it's still developing gives us time to analyze how it's likely to affect us and plan well ahead of time how to handle it -- how to turn it into an opportunity. But if we don't see it coming in time, we'll have to *react* as best we can.

For example, let's think about job security. Most of us spend a big part of our lives working for a living, where "living" means earning enough money to support ourselves and our families. That makes job security an important consideration for most of us.

In years past, the organizations we worked for *were* our job security. We might spend an entire career with one company, and the company's success was our job security. Although our parents and grandparents could depend on their employers for that kind of security, that's no longer possible.

In the increasingly competitive global economy, a company that's successful today may not even exist five years from now. The average life-span of a business organization is now shorter than the working careers of most people.

So for job security, you and I have to rely on the market value of our professions and the demand for our knowledge, skills, and abilities. And we can't even be sure the kind of work we're doing today will still be in demand five or ten years from now. What can we do about it?

We have two choices: do nothing and hope our employer is one of the rare companies that will still be successful years from now; or start looking for developing trends that are likely to make tomorrow's world different from today's and analyzing how those trends may affect our jobs and our professions.

Foresight is essential. Only by looking into the future will we be able to know what kinds of education, training, and development we will need to keep our skills and abilities valuable and marketable. That's why the security of your future employment and income is in *your* hands, not your company's.

It's up to you to spot the trends that will affect you – nobody else is likely to do it for you -- and the farther ahead you can see them, the better prepared you can be to make sure your future is one of opportunities, not threats.

Looking forward will help you stay on the offensive, creating your own future and avoiding someday finding yourself playing defense in a future that's out of your hands.

You may think it's impossible to predict the future, but that's not entirely true. Of course, it is impossible to *see* the future; but it's possible by looking ahead to see *trends* as they develop and use them to predict well in advance how they might affect you.

Trend-Spotting

<u>What?</u>

Trends are new developments in the world around us -- things that may someday change the way we do things. They are many and varied, like baby-boomers reaching retirement age, people moving to warmer climates, and the ways e-mail, text messaging, Twitter, and Facebook are changing the way you and I communicate.

If we can spot those kinds of changes while they are still developing -- before they begin to have a major effect on us -- we can control the *way* they affect us. If we know what to look for, we can predict what will *probably* happen before it actually does.

Suppose, for example, I throw you a ball, but *without any warning*. When you see it coming, the first thing you'll do is "predict" what you have to do to make sure it doesn't hit you.

You may not know exactly *where* it's going to hit, but as you watch it coming, you will see its trajectory (i.e., trend) and automatically narrow down the possible target area; and the closer it gets, the better you're able to predict exactly where it's going to hit.

So although you can't control what *I* do – you can't keep me from throwing the ball – you can control how *you* respond to it, and give yourself a choice: let the ball hit you, try to catch it, or get out of the way. You do this -- chart the course of the ball and make your decision -- in just a fraction of a second, and you do it instinctively without even thinking about it.

Now think about what will happen if you *don't* see the ball coming – you don't spot that particular trend. If you don't see me throw it, you won't know you're in any danger until it's too late, when the ball hits you.

Because you were taken by surprise, you had no choice -- no opportunity to make a decision. The decision was made *for* you by circumstances -- circumstances that caught you by surprise because you weren't looking. So the trend you did *not* see became a threat instead of an opportunity.

Or consider how, when driving on a two-lane road, you sometimes find yourself behind a slow-moving car, and you'd like to pass it. So you go through a series of calculations to predict whether or not you'll have time to pass without colliding with an oncoming car.

You do this by rapidly analyzing the trends of three cars – yours, the one in front of you, and the oncoming car – then deciding whether to pass or not. And you do this kind of trend-spotting almost without thinking about it.

I demonstrate this to my students by tossing a blackboard eraser to one of them without any warning. I've done this hundreds of times, and no student has ever failed to catch the eraser. Why?

Because they see it coming; they see the trend as it develops. Of course, if I throw it to someone who's asleep, it will be a different story because he or she won't see the trend developing.

Through some combination of experience, perception, attention, and reaction, we have the ability to make this kind of prediction. We do it by observing *trends*: we see what *has* happened ("he's thrown the eraser"), watch what *is* happening ("it's coming right at me"), estimate what *will* happen next ("it's going to hit me"), and respond accordingly ("I'll try to catch it").

We all do this, usually without even thinking about it, which means we're all trend-spotters whether we realize it or not.

But we can only see trends if we *look* for them -- if we watch what's going on in the world around us. Unfortunately, the majority of people don't do that, at least not on purpose, which is why some of us usually know what's going to happen ahead of time while others are caught off guard much of the time.

<u>Why?</u>

Trend-spotting allows us to see what's going on in the world around us so we're better equipped to determine which trends will most likely affect us and which we don't need to worry about. Then we can plan ahead how to use change as an opportunity rather than a threat.

At the same time, people who *don't* look ahead are likely to be surprised and confused by the uncertainty of change and allow circumstances to manage *them* instead of the other way around. Ironically, these are often the same people who complain, "I'm too busy; I don't have time to plan." But it's really the other way around: they are too busy because they don't *take* time to plan.

Managing how you are affected by change requires *believing* you can do something about what's happening around you -- that you don't have to let circumstances control you. And if you *know* how to do it, it's easier to convince yourself that you *can* do it.

It isn't necessary to know *everything* that's going on in the world around you. You need only be concerned with those things that are most likely to affect *you* and what you're trying to do, and that's only a small fraction of everything that's happening out there.

How?

There are many things you can do to spot trends. You can begin by reading newspapers and magazines that give different perspectives on the topics that interest you. Well-regarded daily newspapers (e.g., Wall Street Journal, New York Times, Chicago Tribune, Washington Post) are good sources, as are magazines and trade publications that relate to your profession, your area of expertise, or your interests. Through them, you can stay informed about what's developing in your particular areas of interest.

I keep an eye on areas like changing *demographics*, new *technology*, what's new in *education*, the *workplace*, and the *economy*, and especially what new *laws and regulations* are being considered and how they might affect me and what I'm doing.

Other good sources are the *internet*, the *organizations* you belong to, and *networking* with friends and business associates. It really doesn't matter *how* you observe the world around you -- by reading, watching, or listening. It's just important that you *do* it so you have your personal window on the world.

But one of today's challenges is information-overload: *too much* information. Since there's more information available than we can possibly absorb, how can we determine which of it will be useful and which won't? What kinds of information should we look for? What should we keep, and what should we ignore?

First off, recognize that there's a lot more information we *don't* need than what we *do* need. You should only be concerned with those trends that affect your *plan*, your *goals*, and your *vision*. That means assessing which trends are likely to affect your ability to get the *inputs* you need (e.g., money, time, material) and the value of your *outputs* – the demand for what you do or your products or services.

If you can't get the inputs you need when you need them, you won't be able to do whatever it is you're trying to do. Suppose, for example, your vision is a bakery that specializes in premium cakes. Some of your most important inputs will be the ingredients your recipes call for because if you can't get those ingredients, you won't be able to bake your cakes.

But even if you *do* get your ingredients, you have to make sure enough people buy your cakes to provide the revenue you need to stay in business.

In other words, since trends in the external environment can affect your ability to get the inputs you need and to sell your outputs, spotting trends ahead of time can be critical to your success no matter what you're doing.

But you can take comfort in the fact that you don't have to know *everything* about the external world. Focus your attention on the trends that are most likely to affect your goals and your vision.

Luck

We hear a lot about luck, so it's important to understand what role it plays in our accomplishments: what luck *is*, how it affects (or does not affect) what we're trying to do, and how others view what we accomplish. First off, what is luck anyway? The dictionary defines it as, "The chance happening of good or bad events; fortune."

You've probably heard people say, "He's just lucky!" or "She gets all the breaks!" That's the way some folks show how envious they are when someone else gets a promotion, a new job, or an award of some sort. But if you really think about it, how often are our achievements the result of chance happenings? How often is it just luck? How often do we succeed because we got the "breaks"?

In my experience, it's almost never luck or the breaks that separate successful people from their envious colleagues. Most of the time, our success doesn't come from "chance" or "fortune" but by careful planning and hard work. We make our own luck and create our own breaks. Unfortunately, that's the part most people don't see -- or don't want to see -- or overlook or make light of. They have no idea how hard we "lucky" people really had to work to make our "breaks."

It's seldom the luck of the draw that lets some people succeed while others fail. Most of the time, we succeed because we're willing to do the hard work, take the risks, make the sacrifices, and overcome the obstacles that others aren't willing to tackle. Successful people are those who go the extra mile; do what other people won't; do whatever it takes to make the difference.

Someone once said, "Luck is when preparation meets opportunity," and I couldn't agree more.

Summary

Since the world around us is always changing, success can depend on how well we respond to that change. We all know change is inevitable; we just don't know *what* will change or when or where or how.

But watching trends allows us to see the things that are most likely to affect us as they develop but before they actually begin affecting us. That gives us time to prepare for them in advance and reduce the probability they will cause problems for us.

Foresight, or lack of it, can have a major influence on what you accomplish with your career and your life. Your long-term success will ultimately depend on how well you anticipate and act on trends and events happening in the world around you. Although you cannot control that world, you can spot well in advance the trends that may someday affect you. When you have that kind of window on the world, you can face the future with confidence, knowing that whatever happens, you'll be able to turn threats into opportunities.

In recent years, many businesses have been swept aside by changes they didn't see coming; yet virtually every trend that brings major change is visible for a long time before it begins to affect us – often *years* before.

These trends can be visible to anyone who makes it a point to look. But if you aren't looking, you won't see them. Although we cannot control the outside world, we can spot well in advance the trends that may someday affect us.

So make sure you *manage* how the world affects you. Look for developing trends, decide whether they offer threats or opportunities, then act accordingly, before you're *forced* to. Following are some areas that tend to be major sources of the trends and events that affect us:

- demographics
- the economy
- education
- technology
- the workplace
- the physical environment
- family issues
- globalization
- government/legislation/politics

And remember, luck is seldom the difference between success and failure. Although others may see our successes as luck, we usually succeed through hard work, taking risks, and the foresight that turns one person's threats into another's opportunities.

"Shallow men believe in luck."
(Ralph Waldo Emerson, 1803-1882)

Don O'Neal

12. FOCUS

"In the long run
men hit only what they aim at."
(Henry David Thoreau, 1817-1862)

From our discussion in the previous chapter, you should now have a good idea of how and where to look for opportunities. Perhaps you have your vision in mind, and you're ready to line up your goals and start making things happen. That's when focus becomes essential.

Focus means keeping your eye on a single target and avoiding distractions. With so many things in our daily lives competing for our attention, it's hard to concentrate on just one, but that's what you have to do to follow your vision. Focusing on one thing at a time will concentrate your attention and efforts.

So you have to decide what's most important to you and focus on it, meanwhile trying to ignore everything else. Of course, there will be times when something is more important than your vision -- your family, for instance – but beyond those, you should not allow any kind of interruption to distract you or waste your time. Following are some factors to take into consideration as you try to prioritize your obligations and desires to make the most of your time.

Goals

After you've decided which opportunity to focus on, you'll need to set goals: identify the things you have to accomplish to achieve your vision. Your goals are your expectations, your personal commitments, so be sure you set them high.

Most people take pride in being *good* at what they're doing, but every organization has a few *outstanding* performers -- people who are *better* than good, not because they are smarter or more talented than their peers, but because they accomplish more. How? By setting the *right* goals and having *higher expectations* for themselves.

You, too, can be an outstanding performer by doing just those two things: always make sure you're working on what's most *important* -- your highest-priority goals -- and always work at your highest level of *performance*. That's all it takes -- work on the *right* things, and work *hard* – to stand out from the crowd.

Setting the *right* goals means identifying what's most important. But how do we *know* what's most important -- what goals to set?

First we have to identify what has to be done to reach our vision. If we look at vision as a destination – someplace we'd like to be -- our goals become the major things we'll have to accomplish to get there, the mile-markers we'll have to reach along the way.

Linda's dream, her vision, was to go to college. But after graduating from high school, she accepted a full-time job and almost before she knew it had become a working mother. But through the years she never lost sight of her dream, and when her youngest child left the nest, she decided to finally pursue it.

She knew she needed to do two things before she could be admitted: decide *what* field to study, and meet the qualifications for enrollment in that field. So those became her first two goals. While one was straightforward – making a choice between the different fields of study – she found the second more difficult.

Because she was deficient in two of the core requirements, she would have to take and pass two remedial courses before she could be admitted, so completing those courses became her next two goals.

Although that delayed her official enrollment by several months, she successfully completed both courses and was allowed to enroll for the following semester. But now she had to make another decision: should she be a full-time student or part-time?

With children in college, Linda knew she'd still need the income from her full-time job, so she decided to become a part-time student, taking just

Don O'Neal

two courses each semester, instead of the usual five. So her first-semester goals became successfully completing her first two college-level courses.

Focusing on just two goals – her two courses that semester - allowed her to pass both courses with flying colors and gave her the confidence to attempt three courses the next semester. So she increased from two goals to three and successfully completed all three courses. She decided that three was enough – even one more course would overload her -- so three courses became her schedule from that point on.

Although at first it had seemed like just two or three courses at a time would be a slow process, the semesters flew by. And just a few short years later, Linda put on her cap and gown and proudly marched in the graduation processional – one of the proudest days of her life. She had achieved her dream by patiently focusing on just two or three goals at a time.

It's important to describe each goal as an *outcome*, or result, *not* an action. In our example, Linda needed to successfully pass certain courses in order to graduate, so each course became a goal. But when listing them as goals, the wording is important. For example, "Successfully complete (pass) BUS 101 the Fall semester of 2014," *not,* "Take BUS 101 the Fall semester of 2014."

The difference? The first statement has the goal as a result – it has already been accomplished – while the second sees it as an action – I will do it.

That's because you have to *set* goals and make them measurable before you can act on them. We have to know the *result* we want before we can decide *how* to accomplish it.

After you've set goals, you'll need to *prioritize* them: rank them in order of their importance to your vision. That's how you'll know what has to be done first, second, and so on. Prioritizing helps you work on your goals one at a time and constantly reminds you which are most important.

Then, to keep from being distracted by too many goals, you'll need to trim your list down to just a few – one is ideal, but never more than *five*. Any more than that, and you'll be trying to do too many things and risking not getting any of them finished on time.

Our example demonstrates the importance of prioritizing. Linda had to make a decision on which field of study she wanted to pursue before she could know what to do to qualify for enrollment, so her first-priority goal was that decision.

Then she found she'd have to complete two remedial courses before she could enroll as a student in that field, so those became her second and third priorities. She had to complete her first goal – choosing a field – before she could even consider the next one or two.

Finally, every goal must be *measurable:* it has to be quantified (how much) and have a deadline (by when).

Once you've done those four things – decided on your goals, prioritized them, shortened your list, and made them measurable – you're ready to begin working on them; taking *action.* Your goals are your expectations for yourself – your formula for success -- and should be the focus of *all* of your attention and action. And when you do, you'll probably have to make *tradeoffs,* which is often difficult, and can be painful.

Tradeoffs

Whatever we're doing right now must be important or we wouldn't be doing it. But what happens when we want to take on something new -- just add it to what we're already doing? Unfortunately, that sometimes happens, but we shouldn't let it, because the more projects we take on, the less chance we'll have to complete *any* of them on time.

Focusing not only means choosing *what* to do but also what *not* to do. And that can be difficult, because giving up something we've been doing can feel like saying we've been wasting our time. But in reality, when we replace one activity with another, it's just a sign of change; that what we've been doing *was* important, but something else is now *more* important.

For some people, giving up what they've been doing is so hard they just can't do it. So they keep on doing what they've been doing at the same time they're trying to take on new responsibilities. But that never works. It's never possible to do everything we'd like to do or *have* everything we'd like to have, so we have to make tradeoffs. For everything we choose to do or have, there'll be something else we *can't* do or *can't* have, which means we have to give up *something*.

Making tradeoffs isn't easy, but it's absolutely necessary if you want to make the best use of your time and efforts. How you choose to invest your time and energy can make a huge difference in whether or not your vision becomes a reality. And when making choices, deciding what you *won't* do is just as important as deciding what you *will* do. But you won't be able to make the best use of your time if you don't do something about *interruptions*.

Interruptions

I'm sure you know how frustrating it is to be interrupted when you're in the middle of something and how difficult it can be to get back to where you were. Whether you're reading, writing, or just thinking, interruptions disturb your train of thought, break your concentration, and make it difficult -- sometimes impossible -- to recapture your momentum.

There are two kinds of interruptions: by yourself and by someone else. You can control both kinds by setting aside blocks of time when you won't allow interruptions from anyone, including yourself. These should be substantial periods -- ideally four hours or more, but never less than one hour – when you isolate yourself both mentally and socially.

I've found that scheduling my time a week in advance serves two purposes. First, it gives me the peace of mind to ignore everything else on my agenda, because I know that anything that's really important is somewhere on my schedule, so it will get done. Second, scheduling allows me to tell anyone who needs something from me that I can't help them right now, but I will later, and I can tell them exactly *when*. So scheduling solves part of the interruption problem but not all of it; there's also the issue of self-discipline.

It's important for me to have the self-discipline to stick to my schedule. That means telling myself "no" or "not now" whenever I'm tempted to let myself be distracted by things like phone calls, email, or giving in to those who say, "this will only take a minute." Yeah, right!

And you'll have to have that kind of self-discipline, too. Your interruptions, like mine, won't stop until you begin scheduling your time, learning to say "no," and having the fortitude to stick to your schedule. That's why you must always be conscious of what you *should* be working on – what will keep you moving toward your vision -- and what you should pass up.

Summary

Never underestimate the power of focusing your time and efforts. It's amazing what we can accomplish when we've decided something *can* be done and *will* be done, then direct the full force of our efforts to making sure it *does* get done.

Taking advantage of opportunities requires more than just *seeing* them; we have to *do* something about them. There will always be more than one developing trend, and every trend is likely to present a wide range of opportunities, so choosing what to pursue can sometimes seem overwhelming.

You have to narrow down your choices by looking at them from the perspective of your vision: where am I going, and which of these opportunities will be most likely to help me get there?

Then consider the tradeoffs: will this opportunity be a better use of my time and effort than what I'm doing now? If the answer is "yes," you'll have to decide what you've been doing that you'll need to give up to make room for it.

Then you'll need to set goals: what you'll have to accomplish to reach your vision. Setting goals helps focus your efforts and gives you a way of measuring your progress toward your vision.

Note: Portions of this chapter have been excerpted from *Developing Leaders* (O'Neal, 2009: Chapter 5), and from *If Not Now, When?* (O'Neal, 2008: Chapter 7)

Don O'Neal

13. ABILITY

*"A true critic ought to dwell rather
on excellencies than imperfections, ... "*
(Joseph Addison, 1672-1719)

We develop our abilities -- the knowledge and skills that are important to our success -- through education and experience, and they are critical to achieving our goals and realizing our vision. So we need to be well aware of what *strengths* we have and what we're lacking. But that isn't easy, because it's nearly impossible to be objective when thinking about ourselves.

Strengths

Even though you may not be as objective as you'd like, since no one else knows you as well as you know yourself, your own opinion is as good a place as any to begin assessing your strengths. You can start by thinking about what makes you feel most confident. Those are likely to be the things you *like* best, that *interest* you the most, or at which you've been most *successful.*

There are, of course, people who don't believe they *have* any strengths, but they're shortchanging themselves, because *everyone* has strengths. Our strengths may not be obvious, but we *have* them. Yours might be a special talent you take for granted, or something you've been doing so long you don't even think about it.

And there may be areas that don't feel like strengths right now that might be developed into strengths. But if you're not sure if you have any strengths or aren't sure what they are, you may need to get an opinion from someone else.

Other people often notice things about us that we don't. Who should you ask? Begin with those who are closest to you and anyone else who might be affected by what you do or anyone who *expect*s something of you.

That includes family, friends, and business associates: the people who are most likely to see *what* you're doing, *how well* you're doing it, and how well you're meeting their expectations. Ask them to point out what they think are your best points, your personal assets, your strengths. They may see strengths that you don't.

And don't feel you have to be good at everything; nobody is. You only need to be good in those areas that are necessary to reach your goals, and you can get an idea of what they are by answering the following questions about *each* of your goals:

1. What actions will I need to take to reach this goal?

2. What knowledge and skills will those actions require?

3. Are there any of those that I don't have?

4. If so, what do I need to do to develop them?

Whenever we discuss strengths, it's natural to also think about weaknesses. But I don't like the word "weakness"; it sounds too much like "hopeless". So let's think of them as *areas that need improvement*.

Improvement

We all have things we don't do well, don't know how to do, or just aren't able to do, but the only ones we need to worry about are those that may keep us from achieving our goals. So make a list of those and compare it with your answer to the third question under *strengths.*

Then ask yourself, "Will any of them keep me from reaching any of my goals?" If the answer is "yes," you'll need to plan how you can improve in those areas.

Just as there are people who can't see their own strengths, there are some who don't think they have any room for improvement; they see themselves as near-perfect. But *everyone* has areas that could be improved, so if you see yourself as flawless, you really should get a second opinion from someone who knows you well.

They will be more than happy to point out areas in which they feel you should improve, but they'll only tell you if they're convinced that you genuinely *want* to hear what they have to say.

Ask them to point out what they feel are your most vulnerable areas -- your Achilles' heels. If they happen to be the same people you asked about your strengths, they've probably already thought about this.

Then compare their observations with your answer to the third question under *strengths*. Will any of the areas they've pointed out keep you from reaching any of your goals? If so, you'll need to improve in those areas.

And remember, anything that won't keep you from reaching your goals doesn't matter, so you can ignore it.

Distinctive Competence

Although having more than one strength may seem like a good thing, that isn't necessarily so. It might even work against you. Sound confusing? Look at it this way: the more strengths you have, the more things you'll be good at, but the less likely you'll *excel* at any of them.

Remember the old adage, "Jack of all trades; master of none"? Most people who excel do it by focusing on a narrow area of expertise. They don't try to be good at everything; they concentrate on developing and perfecting just one *distinctive competence*.

A distinctive competence is something (some ability) that we do so well it *distinguishes* us -- sets us apart from others. It's something we do better than most other people, so it makes us exceptional. Why is that important?

Suppose you're trying to pursue a particular opportunity, but you know that chances are someone else has seen it, too. That means you will have competition to see who can be first to take advantage of it.

In any competition there are winners and runners-up. Most often the winner has a distinctive competence – something none of the others have – and uses it to be first to solve the problem or satisfy the need.

That means if you can foresee far enough in advance which ability will give you the greatest advantage in achieving your goals, you'll be able to develop a distinctive competence that will give you an advantage over any others who are trying to pursue that same opportunity.

What matters most is being the *best* in the *right area,* not how many strengths you have.

Summary

Recognizing your personal abilities is a key to reaching your goals. To do that, you'll have to compare the knowledge and skills you *have* with those you'll *need* to reach your goals to see if anything is missing. That will point out your development needs: what you'll have to improve before you can reach your goals. And you only have to worry about those that will help you achieve your goals, or keep you from achieving them. None of the others matter.

So after you've determined which abilities are necessary to reach your goals, you can focus on developing distinctive competences – unique talents -- in those areas.

Although we've discussed strengths as the things you *do* best, make sure you don't overlook your personal *values*, *character*, and *reputation*. They can be some of your most valuable assets, or your worst shortcomings.

14. ACTION

"Heaven helps not the men who will not act."
(Sophocles, 495-405 B.C.)

Now that you know how to use your foresight to spot opportunities, how to focus on which opportunity appears most attractive to you, and how to determine what knowledge, skills, and abilities you need to pursue it, it's time to discuss the importance of action.

Once you've set your goals, you'll need to plan exactly how you'll go about achieving them: what actions you'll have to take, and in what order.

Three areas will be critical to achieving your goals: *planning*, *initiative*, and *decisiveness*.

Planning

Developing an action plan is a three-step process: 1) listing the *actions* you'll need to take to achieve each goal; 2) *scheduling* those actions, estimating the time it will take to complete each one, and setting the dates you intend to start and finish them; then 3) determining what *resources* you'll need, when you'll need them, and what you'll have to do to get them.

<u>Actions</u>

Beginning with your highest-priority goal – the one that's most important – you should list *everything* that must be done to reach it: every action, no matter how large or small. Then do the same for the rest of your goals so you'll be able to see if there are any actions that overlap, affect other actions, or serve more than one goal.

It usually takes more than one action to reach a goal, so your final list of all the actions it will take to reach all of your goals is likely to be a long one.

<u>Scheduling</u>

Whenever we're anxious to get something done, the first thing we're likely to think about is how to get it done as quickly as possible. That's okay, but we also have to think about the *order* in which they'll have to be done. While some actions can be taken at any time and in any order, there may be others that have to be done in a certain sequence.

College students, for example, know there are some courses they won't be allowed to take until others -- prerequisites -- have been completed. So they arrange their schedules to take the prerequisites first and the rest of their courses after that.

Once you have what looks like a workable schedule -- a sequence of actions that seems to make sense -- you should estimate how long it will take to complete each one, in *work-hours,* or *work-days*.

Then you can schedule the *dates* you intend to start and finish each action. Those dates can serve as milestones to help you measure your progress and as deadlines to add a sense of urgency to your plan and give you an end-point to look forward to -- your "light at the end of the tunnel."

Once you've finished listing and sequencing your actions and estimating your times and dates, you'll have a tentative calendar that schedules the actions it takes to reach your goals. But that's only part of your plan; you still need to determine what *resources* you'll need, when you'll need them, and how you'll get them.

Resources

Resources include everything -- information, knowledge, skills, equipment, time, and money -- that has to be in place before you can take action. The idea is to make sure you have the resources you need *before* you actually need them. That way, if you should have trouble getting a particular resource, you'll have time to find other sources or to revise your schedule to reflect when the resource *will* be available.

Suppose, for example, one of your actions requires knowledge or skills that you don't currently have (e.g., how to use a new software program) and the date you're scheduled to begin it is just three months away. You realize that's not enough time for you to learn that skill, so you'll have to change your plan.

After thinking about it from all angles, you decide you have two choices: hire someone who has those skills, or reschedule that activity to a later date so you'll have time to learn the skills.

The first option depends on being able to find and hire the right person in the time available at a price you can afford. The second option may appear to be less expensive, but it too has a cost: delaying your schedule.

This kind of dilemma is sometimes unavoidable, but scheduling your activities well in advance will give you time to develop back-up plans for what you will do when something doesn't go as planned. That will ensure that you'll reach your goals in spite of any obstacles that may pop up. That kind of planning requires foresight, but also *initiative*.

Initiative

Initiative simply means taking responsibility for yourself -- doing things on your own without having to be told. Initiative is the difference between people who are self-starters and those who won't take action until someone else pushes them.

Initiative isn't a mysterious talent that some people have and others don't; everyone has it, but not everyone uses it. It takes initiative to follow *your* vision instead of someone else's, but if you wait for someone else to spur you into action, it may never happen; you may never do it. It takes initiative to get the ball rolling and keep moving forward.

Once you've put together a good solid plan, your initiative will make the difference between your vision becoming a reality or remaining just an idle wish. Although lots of people develop plans, most of them remain just hopes because some people just won't take the initiative, and a plan can't put itself into action.

The first step is always the hardest, because we have to overcome inertia (our natural resistance to change), perhaps years of it. Take me, for example.

While writing this, I was a full-time professor with responsibilities that kept me busy at least 40 hours a week. But I am compelled to write; it's important to me. I have thoughts, experience, and information I want to share. So I had to take the initiative to find time to write and ways to work it in around my "real" job.

I finally decided to do my writing early in the day, which meant getting up at 5:00 in the morning. Believe me, getting up while most other people are still snug and warm in bed takes initiative, and it takes it *every day*, not just once in a while.

But I enjoy writing, and I relish the idea that my writing may help other people. For me, that's exciting! Writing is my passion, and it's worth getting up early for. If it weren't, I couldn't do it; I *wouldn't* do it. I wouldn't have the initiative.

If you're passionate about your vision, initiative won't be a problem for you. And once you get started it gets easier, particularly after you begin to feel the satisfaction of the results you'll get (for me, that's a published book). From that point on, your initiative will feed on itself, and you won't have to drive yourself so hard; your sense of accomplishment will do that for you.

Self-Discipline

It takes *self-discipline* to get yourself going and stay on schedule, to have the determination to be the one controlling what you do and when you do it rather than someone or something else. Once you've set your schedule, you must do whatever it takes to stick to it and not allow yourself to be distracted by anyone or anything.

Of course, there will be times when something seems more important than what's on your schedule. When that happens, just make sure it really *is* more important before you let it interrupt your schedule. And whatever you do, don't let yourself get side-tracked just because you hate to say "No".

As we discussed in an earlier chapter, I'm always tempted to give in to requests like, "this will only take a couple of minutes," or "just let me interrupt you for a minute." But when you give in once, it's likely to be followed by a similar request, and another, until your day is shot and you've fallen farther behind schedule.

This seems to happen a lot; perhaps it happens to you. It certainly did to me, and still does, but I no longer give in to it. When it does happen, only self-discipline will keep me, and you, in control of our own time.

Persistence

But initiative by itself isn't enough, nor is self-discipline. It's one thing to get started, but it takes *persistence* to keep moving forward and to stay on course until you achieve your vision. Persistence is the determination to follow through, no matter what you have to do or overcome in the process.

Chapter 3 covered persistence in detail, so there's no need to repeat it here except to remind you that the road to your vision won't always be smooth, it won't always be straight, it won't always be downhill, and you can be sure there will sometimes be obstacles and detours.

It's easy to get where you're going when everything goes according to plan, but things *don't* always happen as planned, and that's when some people just give up and turn back.

But those with persistence keep going; they work around the obstacles; they find a way; they won't give up on their vision no matter what happens. They know that's what it takes to get where they want to go. There will always be obstacles and detours, but persistence will always find a way.

In the worst of conditions, you may even have to abandon your quest for a while. But when you persist, those setbacks will only be temporary, not permanent. I've known quite a number of students who came back to complete their education after being out of school for years. For one reason or another, they had to sidetrack their vision for a while but never gave up on it. Their plans may have been delayed, but their persistence ultimately brought them back.

Time-Management

How much you accomplish will depend in large part on how well you manage your time. Time is our most valuable and most limited resource.

Most of us have more demands on our time than we can possibly fulfill, so we have to find ways to focus on those things that are most important to *us*. By consciously managing your time, you can be much more effective than most other people.

Of course, when you work for an organization, your time isn't your own: it belongs to your boss. Each of us is hired for a reason -- to provide some kind of service -- and your boss is the one who evaluates how well you're using the time she's paying you for.

Now, realistically, your boss can't watch you every minute or every hour, not even every day. So it's largely up to *you* to control how you use your time. A good boss evaluates performance *not* by *how* you do your job but by your *results*: what you accomplish with your time.

When it comes to you personally taking the action necessary to realize your vision, it will be up to you to make sure you use your time effectively.

Here is a three-step process that works:

1) *Record* your time: know where every hour goes;

2a) *Manage* your time: ask questions -- Does this (still) need to be done? Can it be delegated to someone else?

2b) Eliminate time-wasters: lack of foresight, laziness, procrastination, being disorganized, socializing, meetings, information – incorrect, lack of, etc. -- unscheduled "visitors."

3) *Schedule* your time: keep a time-log, prioritize your work, schedule your time in large chunks, set deadlines for yourself.

Initiative can give you the self-discipline, persistence, and time-management skills to keep you moving forward, but you'll need *decisiveness* to make sure you're taking the *right* actions.

Decisiveness

Decisions are about solutions: choosing which course of action will lead to the best outcome. Decisiveness entails making effective decisions and making them in a timely manner.

Most decisions fall into one of two categories: a *choice* between two or more options and a *problem* that needs to be solved.

We make dozens of *choices* every day, like what to wear, which road to take to work, and what to eat for lunch, and here's the process we use, even though we may not think about it at the time:

Make sure we understand the *situation* at hand; consider the possible *choices; decide* which choice to pursue; and take *action – do* it.

Ideally, you would answer five questions before taking action:

1) What is the *situation*?
2) What *choices* do I have?
3) Which looks like the best or most practical *choice*?
4) *Why* do I prefer it?
5a) *How will I know if it works*?
5b) What *result* do I expect?

Although we aren't faced with *problems* nearly as often as with choices, when we do, it's likely to require more thought and effort, such as what to do when your car won't start, or when you have a toothache or when you're stranded without a ride. Here's the process we use, although some of us are much better problem-solvers than others:

Make sure we understand the *problem;* identify the underlying *cause*(s) of the problem; consider possible *solutions; decide* which solution to pursue; and take *action - do* it.

This time you should answer six questions before taking action:

1) What is the *problem*?
2) What is *causing* the problem?
3) What are possible *solutions*?
4) Which of them looks like the *best* or most practical *solution*?
5) *Why* is it best?
6a) *How will I know if it works*?
6b) What *result* do I expect?

Although we like to think we make decisions through a logical, step-by-step process that leads to the one best solution – the optimal decision – that's rarely the case.

That process, called *rational* decision-making, would require analyzing the situation and possibly its underlying causes, considering *all* of the possible solutions, then selecting the *best* course of action: the one that's most rational, or logical.

Although that may seem like the ideal way of making decisions, in reality, we rarely do it that way, for two reasons. First, we seldom have enough time to consider *every* alternative.

Second, our *short-term* memory only allows us to think about a small number of possible solutions at the same time. Comparing alternate solutions requires us to process information, and we humans can only handle a small amount of information at a time.

That's why we usually don't make optimal decisions. Instead, we make decisions that are *acceptable* based on a small amount of readily-available information. This kind of decision may not give us the *best* solution, but it will give us one that's *good enough* to be effective in accomplishing what we need in order to move toward a particular goal.

Information

Although our short-term memory is quite limited, our long-term or *subconscious* memory is huge -- so big, in fact, it's believed to retain everything we've ever seen, heard, read, felt, smelled, or experienced. It's like a massive data bank that has the capacity to store an almost unlimited amount of information. But unfortunately, we don't have much control over it, so our subconscious won't always give us the information we need *when* we need it.

For example, I suspect that like me, you are sometimes embarrassed by not remembering somebody's name, but later it just pops into your mind. That's a good example of how our subconscious works: it's always there and always working, but not necessarily on demand or on *our* schedule.

Since we can't always tap into that magnificent store of information when we need it, we rely on our *conscious* or *short-term* memory most of the time. But it can't process as much information, so most of the time we have to settle for a decision-making process that's *acceptable* rather than optimal.

Instead of considering all possible solutions, we look at a few, one by one, until we have more than one that look as though they could work. Then we stop searching and begin reviewing those we've set aside, finally selecting what we feel is the best of that group. Although that may not lead to the best solution, it usually gives us one that's *good enough* to satisfy our needs at the moment.

Consider, for example, how we choose what to wear each day. At one extreme is the person who doesn't like to make decisions, so he buys only white shirts and dark slacks.

That makes his decision easy -- any shirt will go with any pair of slacks – and saves him a few minutes every day, probably reducing his frustration level as well. (And he may even save money by getting volume discounts when he purchases clothes.) It's said that Albert Einstein used that system and saved additional time by not wearing any stockings.

At the other extreme is the person who has blouses and skirts in a variety of colors. If she has just 12 different blouses and six assorted skirts, she's faced with considering 72 possible combinations.

So how does she choose what to wear? Surely not by thinking about every possible combination; she'd never make it to work. Instead, she probably uses some system, like selecting her blouse first, then the skirt that goes best with it. That allows her to narrow down her choices to just six possible combinations and a manageable decision.

What does all this mean? Simply that when making decisions, we don't usually hold out for the

Don O'Neal

best possible alternative. That takes too much time. Instead, we manage our time by settling for one of the *first* alternatives that looks like it will be an effective solution.

<u>Timing</u>
Although we might find a better solution by searching longer, once we've spent as much time as we feel we can afford, we settle for something we think will work and don't look any further.

But that's okay, because most of the time, *any* decision, even a poor one, is *better* than a *delayed* decision or *no* decision at all. We can waste a lot of time trying to sort through too many alternatives and holding out for the *best* solution. Choosing an *acceptable* solution and implementing it quickly will usually provide a better outcome than waiting to find the *best* alternative.

Even a timely decision has little value if it isn't *implemented* quickly. Timely action gives us an earlier solution and an opportunity to quickly evaluate how well it's working. Then we can take any corrective action that may be necessary, thus reducing the *risk* of a less-than-ideal decision.

<u>Risk</u>
The more decisions we make, and the faster we make them, the more opportunity there is for mistakes or wrong decisions. On the other hand, mistakes are how we learn, so we should never let fear of mistakes keep us from making decisions. We should focus instead on learning from our mistakes.

I am convinced that nobody *wants* to make a mistake.

If you can accept that premise, you can be confident of two things: first, whenever a person makes a mistake, he will learn from it; and, second, it's unlikely he will ever make the same mistake again.

People who won't admit their mistakes or won't reconsider decisions that aren't working can run into major problems. They are potential victims of *escalating commitment*: continuing to invest resources in a failing effort, even when it's obvious it isn't working. An example is the gambler who is losing but keeps doubling his bets, hoping for one win that will recoup all of his losses.

A major cause of escalating commitment is pride. It's easy to become trapped by your unwillingness to admit a bad decision, so you continue investing time, effort, and money trying to salvage the situation and prove your decision was right after all.

People driven by escalating commitment may fear that changing their minds or decisions will be seen as inconsistency or indecisiveness. We often see this in organizations where change is seen as threatening. In that kind of culture, people may be afraid of being seen as "wishy-washy" if they don't stick with their original decisions. They do whatever it takes to make it look like their decision was right in the first place.

There's also the pressure of *sunk costs*. The more time, effort, and especially money we invest in a decision, the more we're committed to that course of action and to doing whatever will make us feel it wasn't wasted.

One way to avoid the high cost of escalating commitment is to identify in advance the point at which we will abandon a decision -- the point at which its probability of success will be in serious doubt.

Then we must have enough self-discipline to, when we reach that point, get out or change course no matter how much we have invested or how much it hurts our pride. Rather than focusing on how much we've lost, we should think in terms of how much we'll *save* by not continuing to invest in a losing effort.

An organizational culture that tolerates mistakes is a good way of reducing the risk of escalating commitment, and the same approach can be used by you as an individual. When you allow yourself the freedom to revise or reverse less-effective decisions without worrying too much about your "sunk costs," you'll waste less time trying to defend and justify decisions that no longer seem to be working.

Intuition

Our experiences are a major source of the information stored in our subconscious mind, information that can be invaluable when we make decisions. And some of this information can become so firmly embedded in our subconscious that it enables us to make some decisions automatically, without thinking about it; our instincts and reflexes take over for us.

It's interesting to note that these intuitive decisions are often just as good as the decisions we make slowly and deliberately, sometimes even better. That may be because they are made so quickly, based on very little conscious thought, that we don't take time to second-guess ourselves. Our intuition provides information that we may not even realize we have.

That's why it sometimes pays to go with your first impulse and let your subconscious make the decision. This can be one of the best ways of making timely and effective decisions, as long as we monitor the results so we can quickly change or fine-tune the decision if it doesn't turn out as we had hoped.

Research has found that students score better on multiple-choice exams when they stick with their first instinct and worse when they second-guess themselves by going back and changing their answers.

Summary

Planning lets us determine in advance what specific *actions* we'll have to take to achieve our goals and realize our vision. Making sure those actions take place when they're needed and in the right sequence requires careful *scheduling* and determining what *resources* will be needed to put the plan into action.

A plan is only a piece of paper, a pipe-dream, until we do something with it -- take action. And that's where *initiative* is essential, because it's up to *you* to put your plan into action; nobody else can do it for you.

Initiative requires *self-discipline* to keep you focused and avoid distractions, *persistence* to help you overcome any obstacles or detours that get in your way, and *time-management* to ensure the best use of your most valuable resource.

Charles Schwab, an early president of Bethlehem Steel, hired a consultant to show him how to manage his time more effectively. The consultant gave Schwab the following note and told him to follow its advice every day:

'Write down the six most important tasks that you have to do tomorrow and number them in the order of their importance. Now put this paper in your pocket and the first thing tomorrow morning look at item *one* and   start work on it until you finish it. Then do item *two*, and so on. Do this until quitting time and don't be concerned if you have finished only one or two.'

After trying his advice for several days, Schwab was so impressed with the results that he paid the consultant $25,000 for his one-paragraph note during a time when the average American worker made less than $2000 per *year*. (Bluedorn, 2002)

Decisiveness -- the ability and willingness to make effective decisions -- is a critical success factor and one that's often the problem when individuals fail to reach their potential. Decision-making requires assessing what *information* is necessary and what isn't, using that information to make *timely* decisions, and assessing *risk* to determine the tradeoffs and consequences of alternative choices. Effective decision makers have faith in their *intuition* and use it confidently, particularly when time or information is in short supply.

Those three elements – planning, initiative, and decisiveness – usually make the difference between those whose visions become reality and those who just wish and hope.

Note: Portions of this chapter have been excerpted from *Developing Leaders* (O'Neal, 2009: Chapters 6 and 7), and from *If Not Now, When?* (O'Neal, 2008: Chapters 6 and 7)

Don O'Neal

15. COURAGE

*"The courage we desire and prize
is not the courage to die decently,
but to live manfully."*
(Thomas Carlyle, 1795-1881)

Courage – "The quality of mind that enables one to face danger with confidence, resolution, and firm control of oneself …" (*The American Heritage Dictionary)*

But courage isn't limited to *physical* danger. In our day-to-day lives, it often takes courage to overcome our fears of failure, embarrassment, unpopularity, or being seen as different. In addition,

"It is not the courage of the battle, or the courage of crisis, that is of concern… No, the courage that counts is the courage to do your job day by day, quietly, without recognition, often without hope, sustained only by the realization that you are doing something that matters to you and to others. It is the courage to listen and learn from criticism – and to persevere." (Hayes, 1983:42)

That kind of courage takes *choice, commitment*, and *sacrifice*.

Choice

In Chapter 1 we talked about the choices we have in how to lead our lives: let fate make our decisions for us and sit back and let life happen *to* us; or make our own decisions and *choose* the kind of life we want. It's one of the most important decisions you'll ever make.

If you *let* life happen, you won't need courage; all you'll have to do is watch your life unfold. Then whatever good fortune comes your way will be due to luck, and your bad fortune to circumstances beyond your control: "There was nothing I could do."

You'll need courage to take charge of your life; in fact, you'll need courage just to *choose* that way of life. Then you'll need courage to take full responsibility for your decisions – bad and good. It's easy to take the credit when things go right but not so easy when they don't. It takes courage to admit your failures, miscalculations, mistakes, or wrong decisions, then learn from them and move on.

But there's a big payoff: the satisfaction of knowing you're doing something *meaningful* with your life. Meanwhile, those who *let* life happen will be bystanders as life passes them by, regretting the things they *didn't* do, and just *existing* -- not really living.

Choosing to make your life happen won't always be easy; nothing worthwhile ever is. In fact, the value of anything is based on how difficult it is to obtain; the more difficult it is, the higher its value. And it takes *commitment* to make it through the difficult times.

Commitment

Commitment – persistence, dedication, fortitude – is what enables ordinary people to accomplish extraordinary things. But the more difficult the task, the harder it is to find those people – the ones who will take it on and stick with it until it's finished. That's because some people set their expectations by what they *know* they can do. They prefer a "slam dunk" – a sure thing – to anything that looks difficult.

And those who *excel* set high expectations for themselves -- higher than most other people – and commit themselves to doing whatever is necessary to meet those expectations and to overcome any obstacles they encounter along the way.

Commitment makes the difference between starting something and seeing it through to the finish. And the higher the expectations, the more commitment it takes to persevere in the face of frustration, disappointment, and failure.

That's why so few people are willing to take the more difficult path, and why they are so valuable. They are the ones we can depend on not only to set high expectations but also to see them through to completion; they get the job done.

Commitment means taking *responsibility* for your failures and mistakes rather than blaming them on someone else; being willing to *take chances*; and having the confidence to *speak out* -- say what you think.

Speaking out can be especially difficult because of the fear of hurting someone's feelings. That's why we don't always say what we think. We don't *intend* to lie, but when someone asks a question and we're afraid an honest answer will hurt their feelings, we may not tell the truth. And we may come to regret it, as in the following example:

It was a hot Sunday afternoon (104 degrees) in the small Texas town, but a breeze made it almost bearable in the shade of the back porch, where two couples were enjoying cold lemonade. It was a pleasant interlude; that is, until one of the four suggested they drive to Abilene for dinner.

Despite the heat, the distance, and the fact that the only available automobile was not air-conditioned, the four of them got into the car and headed for Abilene.

Here's how one of the participants described what happened next:

"Some four hours and 106 miles later, we returned, hot and exhausted. We sat silently in front of the fan for a long time. Then, to be sociable and to break the silence, I dishonestly said, 'It was a great trip, wasn't it?'

No one spoke. Finally, my mother-in-law said, with some irritation, 'Well, to tell the truth, I really didn't enjoy it much and would rather have stayed here. I just went along because the three of you were so enthusiastic about going.'"

Her honesty opened the floodgates, and the other three quickly admitted none of them had wanted to go either, but hadn't wanted to risk hurting the feelings of the others by speaking out.

The narrator summed it up:

"Here we were, four reasonably sensible people who – of our own volition – had just taken a 106-mile trip across a godforsaken desert in furnace-like heat and a dust storm, to eat unpalatable food at a hole-in-the-wall cafeteria in Abilene, when none of us had really wanted to go. To be concise, we'd done just the opposite of what we wanted to do."

They had all suffered in silence through a miserable ordeal that could have been avoided if just one of them had had the courage to speak out and say, "I don't want to go." Writing about it later, Jerry Harvey called it the *Abilene Paradox*: the tendency of groups of people to agree to things that none of them really wants because none of them has the courage to say how they really feel. (1988:14)

Sacrifice

Seldom is anything worthwhile accomplished without sacrifice. Because we can't have everything we'd like to have and can't do everything we'd like to do, we're constantly making sacrifices even though we may not think of them as sacrifices. But most choices we make are tradeoffs, where choosing one thing usually means giving up something else.

When we do that, we may not think of it as sacrificing because we're doing it for *ourselves.* But when we are faced with giving up something *now* in exchange for something we won't get until *later*, perhaps much later, we get a better idea of what sacrificing means.

For example, when young people graduate from high school, they have to decide whether or not to go on to college. They know that college will involve major sacrifices in time, money, effort, and perhaps even fun, so skipping college, getting a job, and starting to enjoy life right now can look a lot more attractive.

The lure of instant gratification makes college look like a huge sacrifice for a goal that's a long way off. A degree will take at least four years of working and worrying and will cost thousands of dollars – money that may take years to repay.

It can seem much easier to give up on the idea of college and start living the good life right now. Why, then, does anyone choose to *go* to college?

We do it when we believe we'll be better off in the long-run -- that a college degree will give us a better life, for the *rest* of our life. Only then will we consider trading short-term enjoyment for such a long, hard road. It's a big sacrifice but one many feel is a key to future success:

"Any time you see success, you can be sure someone made sacrifices to make it possible." (Maxwell, 2007:226)

To this point, we've focused on the kind of sacrifices we make for *ourselves*. It's easy to understand why we do that, but why are some people willing to make sacrifices for others when they expect nothing in return? They do it because they're *unselfish;* they don't just think about themselves, but feel a duty -- a responsibility -- to others.

Those are the people who are willing to make the *hard* decisions -- the kinds of decisions we all face from time to time. By *hard* decisions I mean what are referred to as *right* decisions: decisions that will benefit *everyone,* not just a privileged few. Why do we call them *hard* decisions?

Because they're sure to be unpopular with some people, and *never* popular with everybody, so we make them realizing they're likely to upset a lot of people and make us unpopular with them.

It's easy to get lured into "popularity traps" and make decisions based on how many people will like them -- decisions that won't make too many people unhappy. Those kind of decisions are usually the *wrong* decisions, because they seldom face the important issues, yet we make them to avoid the discomfort of challenging the status quo.

So make sure you understand up front that making the *right* decisions – the hard decisions -- will make you *unpopular* with some people, perhaps *most* people. But if you let your decisions be influenced by whether or not they'll affect your popularity, you'll be selling your soul to feed your ego.

As difficult as that may be – we hate the thought of people not liking us – we should never let popularity or consensus influence our decisions. The *right* decisions may not result in the best outcome for ourselves, but they will benefit those who depend on us and who look to us as examples.

Summary

Where do people find the courage to make the choices, commitment, and sacrifices that are in the best interests of those who depend on them, regardless of how it may affect their own lives?

Here are four tips to help people find courage within themselves:

1) *"Believe in a higher purpose"* – Those "who have a strong emotional commitment to a larger vision or purpose find the courage to step through fear."

2) *"Draw strength from others"* – "Love is a strong ingredient of courage, because it makes us willing to sacrifice."

3) *"Welcome failure"* – "Know that failure can lead to success and that the pain of learning strengthens [us]."

4) *"Harness frustration and anger"* – "Sometimes outrage over a perceived injustice can give a mild-mannered person the courage to confront...." "Anger, in moderate amounts, is a healthy emotion that provides energy to move forward. " -- (Daft, 2008:184-186)

In his book, *The Courage to Be*, Paul Tillich describes courage as the willingness to sacrifice elements that are important to us, --like pleasure, happiness, and even life itself -- in order to fulfill the highest purpose of our lives, or as he puts it, "the attainment of the highest good." (1952:7)

However we define it, and however we practice it, courage is what makes the difference between living a meaningful life and merely existing.

Note: Portions of this chapter have been excerpted from *Developing Leaders* (O'Neal, 2009: Chapter 8.)

Don O'Neal

AFTERWORD

"I believe that every right implies a responsibility;
every opportunity, an obligation;
every possession, a duty"
(John D. Rockefeller, Jr., 1874-1960)

While reading through this book for the first time (and I hope it won't be the *last*), you've probably noticed how often I've used the word *responsibility*. If there's any single word that can summarize the message of this book, that's the one.

To me, there are few things more important than responsibilities. They help shape our lives: they define us, drive us, sometimes frustrate us, but in the long run, they *inspire* us. Our responsibilities are a big part of what makes us who we are and what makes our lives *meaningful*.

The title, *If Not You, Who?* is asking you to consider, "If *you* don't take responsibility for your life, *who will?*" And there are only two possible answers: either *nobody* will, or *somebody else* will.

If *nobody* takes responsibility for your life, you're likely to spend it adrift on a sea of complacency, not knowing where you're going or how or what you'll find when you get there.

179

There's a good chance you'll wind up living a life of regret, never really knowing where you are, why you're there, and why you're not happy -- not a very pleasant prospect for most people.

Then you could let *someone else* take charge of your life *for* you. That would be an easy out; you wouldn't have to worry about making decisions, and it may be better than drifting through life. You might even have a purpose, but it would probably be someone else's purpose -- their idea of where you should go, what you should do, and how you should do it.

At least that way, your life may have some meaning, even though it might not be *your* meaning. You may enjoy not having to worry about responsibilities, but would that kind of life make you happy? Would it be meaningful, satisfying, rewarding? Only you can answer that one.

But if you've read this far, you're probably not the kind of person who would settle for either of those scenarios, so you're more likely to answer, "It will be me. I'll take responsibility for my own life." And once you've made that choice, your life will take on new meaning.

You'll be ready to go through the book again, concentrating first on Part I, Purpose – to make sure you understand what responsibility *to yourself* really means. Then you'll move on to Part II, Integrity – responsibility *for* yourself; Part III, Responsibility – responsibility to *others,* and Part IV, Opportunity – the fun part, where you look toward your future and begin making it happen.

Taking responsibility for your life will take courage, but it will be worth whatever you have to go through, as I found at a point in my career when I was offered a dream job with another company.

Of course, a job offer is a good thing, but as with any major change, it presented me with several major concerns:

1) Having been with my present company for 14 years, I was just one year short of vesting in the company's retirement plan, and I'd lose all of it.

2) I was earning three weeks' vacation each year, increasing to four weeks next year, but only two weeks at the new company.

3) I was overseeing the work of 40 people but would only be supervising two in my new job.

4) My current company employed more than 3000 people, had been in business for more than 70 years, and was a leader in its field, while the new company was less than three years old, employed fewer than 50 people, and had yet to make a profit, so it's future was still a big question mark.

Considering all I'd be giving up, why would I call this new position a "dream" job? Because I could see more career opportunities at this startup, if it survived. And because those who were recruiting me believed I had unique knowledge and experience that would be invaluable in helping their company grow.

With all I'd be risking, what would I do if the new company *didn't* survive? I agonized long and hard about whether to go or stay. If the offer had come a year later, the decision would have been easier, but by that time this opportunity would be gone.

After weeks of back-and-forth debate with myself, I finally accepted the offer, rationalizing that if I didn't take it and the new company *did* succeed, I'd be kicking myself for years to come about the missed opportunity.

It was a gamble, as many opportunities are, but this one turned out really well for me. The new company did succeed and gave me career opportunities I couldn't have even imagined with my previous employer. It was one of the most difficult decisions I've ever made, but one of the best.

And that was just one of several opportunities that came my way over the years. Although each one was different, they all had the same three challenges:

1) They seemed to come along at the worst most inconvenient times.

2) They involved considerable risk.

3) They required sometimes painful tradeoffs. So opportunities always have a cost -- sometimes a very high cost. But nothing worthwhile is ever easy, or without sacrifice.

So whenever you see an opportunity, don't be shocked if it shows up at the worst possible time. Never let that be the deciding factor in whether to take it or not. Think hard about what you stand to gain, not just what you'll have to give up.

It takes courage and self-confidence to take that kind of risk and make those kinds of tradeoffs – to step out of your comfortable rut and take a chance. But that's usually the difference between those who *do things* and those who only *wish* they had.

I hope you enjoy your journey as much as I've enjoyed mine. And remember, I'll be with you all the way. Any time you have questions, concerns, comments, or suggestions, feel free to send them to *doneal1010@gmail.com.*.

Don O'Neal

REFERENCES

Bauby, J-D., 1997, *The Diving Bell and the Butterfly,* New York: Random House

Bennis, W., Nanus, B., 1985, *Leaders: The Strategies for Taking Charge,* New York: Harper & Row

Bluedorn, A. C., 2002, *The Human Organization of Time,* Stanford, CA: Stanford Business Books

Czikszentmihalyi, M., 1990, *Flow: The Psychology of Opimal Experience,* New York: Harper Perrenial

Daft, R. L., 2008, *The Leadership Experience,* Mason, OH: Thomson/South-Western

Harvey, J. B., 1988, *The Abilene Paradox and Other Meditations on Management,* New York: Lexington Books

Hayes, J. L., 1983, *Memos for Management: Leadership,* New York: American Management Association

Kohn, A., 1986, *No Contest: The Case Against Competition,* Boston: Houghton Mifflin

Kouzes, J. M., Posner, B. Z., 2007, *The Leadership Challenge,* San Francisco: Jossey-Bass

Don O'Neal

Maslow, A. H., 1998, *Maslow on Management,* New York: John Wiley & Sons

Maxwell, J. C., 2007, *The 21 Irrefutable Laws of Leadership,* Nashville: Thomas Nelson

O'Neal, D., 2008, *If Not Now, When?,* Bloomington, IN: AuthorHouse

O'Neal, D., 2009, *Developing Leaders,* Boston: American Press

Rokeach, M., 1973, *The Nature of Human Values,* New York: The Free Press

Tillich, P., 1952, *The Courage to Be,* New Haven: Yale University Press

Wellner, A. S., 2005, "Lost in Translation", *Inc. Magazine,* September: 37-38

Wright, R., 2000, *Nonzero: The Logic of Human Destiny,* New York: Vintage Books

ABOUT THE AUTHOR

Donald E. O'Neal, MBA, Ph.D., is Professor of Management, Emeritus, at the University of Illinois Springfield, and a visiting professor in the China Executive Leadership Program at the University of Illinois at Urbana-Champaign, teaching Strategic Management, Leadership, Human Resource Management, and Organization Design.

After a successful business career (executive positions in Engineering, Sales, and Vice President of Human Resources), he completed his doctorate in Strategic Management at the University of Illinois, Urbana/Champaign, in 1995.

He is co-editor of six volumes of strategic management research papers (John Wiley & Sons, London, UK), and is the author of four previous books: *Managing Strategically* (2003,2005, 2008,) *Developing Leaders* (2009,) and *People in Organizations* (2010,) all published by American Press, Boston,) and *If Not Now, When?* (available through Amazon.)

Dr. O'Neal conducts seminars, workshops, and strategic planning sessions for corporate, not-for-profit, and governmental organizations.

Don O'Neal